OPTIONS TRADING FOR BEGINNERS

Options Trading for Beginners: The Easiest Guide To Start Creating Your Passive Income Step By Step, Using The Best Proven Strategies Out There

© Copyright 2020 - All rights reserved.

The content contained within this book may not be reproduced, duplicated or transmitted without direct written permission from the author or the publisher.

Under no circumstances will any blame or legal responsibility be held against the publisher, or author, for any damages, reparation, or monetary loss due to the information contained within this book. Either directly or indirectly.

Legal Notice:

This book is copyright protected. This book is only for personal use. You cannot amend, distribute, sell, use, quote or paraphrase any part, or the content within this book, without the consent of the author or publisher.

Disclaimer Notice:

Please note the information contained within this document is for educational and entertainment purposes only. All effort has been executed to present accurate, up to date, and reliable, complete information. No warranties of any kind are declared or implied. Readers acknowledge that the author is not engaging in the rendering of legal, financial, medical or professional advice. The content within this book has been derived from various sources. Please consult a licensed professional before attempting any techniques outlined in this book.

By reading this document, the reader agrees that under no circumstances is the author responsible for any losses, direct or indirect, which are incurred as a result of the use of information contained within this document, including, but not limited to, errors, omissions, or inaccuracies.

TABLE OF CONTENTS

INTRODUCTION **6**
    What Kind of Investor Are You? 6
    How Much Time Can You Learn It? 10
    How Realistic Is Getting Rich in Investing? 14
    How to Be a Winning Trader While Everyone Else Loses 15

CHAPTER 1: OPTION BASICS FOR BEGINNERS **22**
    What Are Options? 22
    How Do Options Work? 22
    What Is an Option Contract? 24
    Other Types of Options 25
    Know the Lingo 26
    Understanding Pricing Influences 28
    Why You Should Trade Options 29
    Disadvantages 30
    Types of Options 31
    Going Long vs. Going Short 33
    Financial Leverage 34
    How to Start Trading Options 37
    In and Out of the Money 38
    When Is an Option Liquid? 39
    Leverage and Options Trading 40
    Buying and Selling Options 40

CHAPTER 2: TRADING FUNDAMENTALS **42**
    Entry into the Options Trading Market 43
    Technical Indicators You Need to Know About 45
    Upward Trend 48
    Downward Trend 48
    Sideways Trend 48
    Creating Your Watch List for Possible Positions 52
    Candlestick Charts and Patterns 54
    Rules for Successful Trading 58
    Things That Affect the Price of Options 68
    Tips for Success 69
    Identifying a Reliable Broker 74
    Types of Brokers 75

CHAPTER 3: QUICK AND ACCURATE BASICS OPTION TRADING STRATEGIES 78
- LONG CALLS 78
- SHORT CALL OPTIONS STRATEGY 80
- LONG PUTS/BUYING PUT OPTIONS STRATEGY 82
- ALTERNATIVE REPAIR STRATEGY 83
- COMBINED REPAIR STRATEGY 83
- CONSIDER THE STRIKE PRICE 84
- TIME TO UNWIND 85
- COVERED CALL STRATEGY 86
- BULL CALL STRATEGY 86
- BEAR PUT SPREAD 88
- CALENDAR PUT SPREAD 93
- NAKED CALL SHORTING 97
- THE BEAR CALL SPREAD 97
- SHORT PUT/SELLING PUT OPTIONS STRATEGY 103
- THE IMPORTANCE OF VOLATILITY 104

CHAPTER 4: ADVANCED STRATEGIES 108
- MARRIED PUT 108
- THE STRADDLE AND THE STRANGLE 109
- PROTECTIVE COLLAR 114
- THE IRON CONDOR 116
- IRON BUTTERFLY 122

CHAPTER 5: OPTION TRADING AND STOCK TRADING 124
- WHY USE STOCK MARKET STRATEGIES? 124
- INVESTMENT STRATEGIES 127
- STOCK MARKET STRATEGIES AND MONEY MANAGEMENT 128
- GUIDE TO INVESTING IN STOCKS 130

CHAPTER 6: TAKE CONTROL OF YOUR MONEY 144
- MONEY & RISK MANAGEMENT TECHNIQUES 144
- RISK MANAGEMENT 145

CHAPTER 7: TRADING PSYCHOLOGY 152
- AN OPTIONS TRADING MINDSET 152

CONCLUSION 160

INTRODUCTION

Options allow you the right, but not the obligation, to purchase something at a later date while paying today's prices. They can be based on many different assets and, there are many strategies that you will be able to use in order to see success with options that it makes sense why so many people would choose this as their investment.

This guidebook is going to take some time to talk about options trading and how it works. We will start with some of the basics that come with options, such as how they work, what they are all about and the benefits of trading these rather than working with some other investment types. We will then move on to some of the best strategies that you can go with when trading options, and how you can pick a good strategy that will help you to earn a profit, no matter how the market is doing.

When you are ready to start making some money with options and you want to learn the right way to do it to reduce your risks and actually make some money, then take the time to look through this guidebook to help you get started.

What Kind of Investor Are You?

Long or short-term investor?

While they are polar opposites, going long and going short both describe the state of ownership of the asset associated with the option. Going short is also known as having a short position. It describes the state of the seller, not owning the asset associated with the option. Going long is also described as having a long position. It means that the seller owns the asset associated with the option.

There is another application of long and short positions that is applied to both call and put options. Having a long call option means that the trader expects the price of the asset to go up so that he or she can benefit. The opposite is true for having a long-put option. The trader expects the price of the asset to depreciate so that he or she can exercise the right to sell the option at the strike price.

As you can see, neither of these options refer to the period associated with that option. Rather, the focus is on the ownership of the associated asset. As such, the person who owns the asset is called the long position holder. If this person expects the price of the asset to rise, then this is called having a bullish view. This applies to a trader holding a long call option.

If this person expects the price of the asset to fall, this is known as having a bearish view. This is the scenario where a trader has a long put option.

Plenty of advice exists for investing in retirement or other long term visions. There is also plenty of advice on savings accounts for goals in the shorter term, like saving for an upcoming vacation next summer. But what if your goals fall in between these two?

The difference between long and short term goals:

When your goals are over 10 years away, you are able to take on risk and invest in stocks to reach better potential for returns. You will have time to adjust accordingly, if needed, by saving more money or by shifting your goal a bit. People also opt for long term investing because the stock market has a tendency to go up over time periods. This is not possible with short term goals.

Long-term goal considerations:

Is the long term always a safer choice? If these benefits exist from the quality of the market in the past, does this mean that they always will? No, but you are more likely to receive at least a portion of a beneficial return from investing in long periods of time rather than opting for a shorter time.

Should you invest it all-in long-term goals?

Does this mean it's wise to place all of your savings into the market? Although some choose to do so, it isn't recommended.

The optimal balance: A smarter choice would be to pick an assortment of investments that allow you to benefit from the upsides of the market and give you protection when the market is falling. It doesn't need to be much more complicated.

A savings account may be better for some: When it comes to shorter periods of time, the money you end up saving is a lot more important than what you might earn in an interest rate. For one, the money is guaranteed. Plus, the amount you earn may not be much more than what you'd earn from the interest in the savings account.

A quality account with interest rates that are competitive:

The best choice is to find an account that gives you good interest rates, considering competition, or even a CD that goes along with your goals and their time frames.

Medium-term goal considerations:

A medium goal is considered to be less than 10 years but more than three. This gives you a variety of choices to make. You could choose to invest part of your savings, hoping that the return you get back will make your long-term goals more possible.

The risk of that idea: Investing money from your savings account might end up making your goal more difficult to accomplish if the market ends up going through something rough.

Less time to recover if something goes wrong:

Unlike longer-term goals, medium goals don't give you as much time to recover from unexpected issues in the market.

There is no objective answer for medium investing goals. It has more to do with your personality and specifics of your finances than anything else. So, how do you decide what to do?

How to play it safe with these uncertainties:

The uncertainties of the first type: When it comes to goals that involving you needing the capital specifically at some point, even with an undefined date, you should always be conservative with your money. In cases like this, it's better to know for sure that you have capital waiting when the need arises rather than attempting to earn a return that is slightly higher and not even a certain event.

The uncertainties of the second type: The goals of the second variety give you a bit more freedom with engaging in risk. Since you don't need the capital on a specific date, you will be able to strive for returns that are higher without the risk of it coming back to haunt you later. Obviously, being able to take this chance doesn't necessarily mean it's the wisest decision.

Are you in need of higher returns?

Considering the length of time that must elapse between right now and the time when your goal is reached; the capital you have put into savings, and the extra money you put into savings regularly, what type of return are you needing?

Perhaps you don't need more than what is possible from a CD or savings fund online. If this applies to you, is it worth the trouble of risking having a lower savings account that you will need in the future?

Is it worth watching the value of your account go down?

Even if you are capable of taking on a great deal of risk, this doesn't mean that you have to do it. Deciding to place money into stocks, even in small amounts, is deciding to subject your capital to the downs and ups that come along with that. Of course, we all enjoy the ups and dislike the downs, which can be quite substantial at times. A great rule to follow is to assume that during any period of 12 months, you could lose up to half of the capital you invested in stocks. You could also assume that you would be able to recover from that, but when it comes to short periods, it may be harder to do.

Whether you are interested in the long, medium, or short-term goals, you should ask yourself some questions and take time to answer them. Think about these for a while before giving your answer.

Remember why you are investing in the first place:

People are often bored with the idea of using a savings account, but even the most experienced of investors should have one since having guaranteed money is better than having no funds guaranteed.

Remember that people invest because they need extra money and risking it all on a chance of earning is not smart. Only you can decide what works best for you.

How Much Time Can You Learn It?

Don't expect yourself to do well just from the get-go. It can happen, but it is rare. There will be a steep learning curve where you will see some gains and losses. But do not be discouraged. Keep at it.

More importantly, you should be long-term focused. You should expect that it will take some time before you rule like a pro. Look, it's like learning guitar. You won't be playing the solo from Stairway to Heaven anytime soon, but with practice, you will surely improve. Think of trading like that. It is like learning

Do your homework daily

Get up early and study the financial environment before the market opens and look at the news. This allows you to develop a daily options trading plan. The process of analyzing the financial climate before the market opens is called pre-market preparation. It is a necessary task that needs to be performed every day to asset competition and to align your overall strategy with the short-term conditions of that day.

An easy way to do this is to develop a pre-market checklist. An example of a pre-market checklist includes but is not limited to:

- Checking the individual markets that you frequently trade options in or plan to trade options in to evaluate support and resistance.
- Checking the news to assess whether events that could affect the market developed overnight.
- Assessing what other options traders are doing to determined volume and competition.
- Determining what safe exits for losing positions are.
- Considering the seasonality of certain markets are some as affected by the day of the week, the month of the year, etc.

Options Trading Time Frames

Time frames are an integral part of trading options and need to be given careful consideration when initiating any investment. Essentially, time frames are represented with charts, such as those that will be outlined in the next chapter. There are countless time frames, as they can range from as short as one hour to several months long. It is up to the investor to analyze the time frames in order to predict how the market will move, and thus if the investor needs to sell or buy options.

So what exactly needs to be analyzed? That would be the trendline, which is detailed in the time frame chart. By looking at the chart, an investor will be able to tell if it is bearish or bullish in nature and, using the trade signals discussed in the next chapter, when the market is going to continue or reverse its trend. However, there is not just one trend that investors need to be concerned with. There are actually three trends: primary, intermediate, and short term.

Every underlying security can be represented with these trends, which are reliable depending on the length of their time frame. Having a longer time frame allows investors to track the trend of an underlying stock more accurately. Take, for example, a 3-month long time frame versus a 5-minute time frame. The 5-minute frame would only show a very small portion of the asset's trend, which may be an abnormality when taking a longer time frame trend into account or even may be plain inaccurate, depending on how much noise is occurring in regard to that particular asset. Thus, since a long-term trend is more reliable, it is the most accurate for locating the primary trend.

The primary trend should always be the investor's main concern. This is not because it is the only one worth paying attention to. On the contrary, different trends will be used by different types of investors, such as a day trader versus a position trader. In the case of the position trader, it would be wise to make the primary trend a priority because it focuses on long-term time frames and then makes smaller profits using the intermediate-and short-term frames. In juxtaposition to this, a day trader would mainly use the primary trend as an umbrella for the short-term time frame he or she would mostly work with as calls and puts are swiftly traded. It is, therefore, the best for a beginning investor to concentrate on the work he or she would most like to do and then find the appropriate time frame for it, always basing calculations off of the primary trend. This can be achieved by using the short-term trend in correlation with the faster time frame and the investor's preferred time frame for the intermediate trend, all while tracking the primary trend in the long-time frame.

In line with the idea of tailoring time frames and securities to an investor's personal preference, the two-time frames not chosen as the investor's primary concern should be used to complement the primary time frame. Depending upon how the investor chooses to utilize the time frames, the investor could potentially reap the rewards on three separate levels, enacting many of the strategies discussed in the previous chapter. For example, an investor may hold a long position on a stock using the primary trend to predict movements within the market for that particular underlying investment, also known as the underlying trend. Once this has been identified, the investor uses whatever time frame is most suited to his or her style of trading (short for day trading, long for position trading, etc.) in order to determine the intermediate trend pattern. The investor then brings in the short-term trend in order to implement strategies that may fulfill any number of purposes. These may include using the short-term trend and time frame to create insurance for the long position, to reap benefits with calls or puts as the trend fluctuates, or any other of the numerous uses of short-term trends and time frames. How the time frames are utilized is completely up to the individual investor and thus is a flexible way to generate and multiply income using the investor's natural trading strengths.

Because there are time frames containing trends representing all underlying assets, neophyte options traders can often become confused by the contradictory information. Say, for example, the primary trend for the stock of company XYZ in a long-time frame shows the stock is bullish. However, when the investor looks at a short-term trend on a 2-day time frame, the stock appears to be completely bearish with no obvious signs of a rally. The investor should not panic and, begin selling all of his or her shares. Instead, the investor must realize that the short-term trend is merely a small portion of the primary trend, which, if it is a continuation pattern, will keep its bullish outlook and continue climbing the chart. It is easy to see from this example why organization and a clear understanding of options trading before entering the business are priceless tools.

One of the keys to growing a portfolio is concentrating on the future trends of the market rather than the past. Many investors who are either beginners or overly scared of losing money rely purely on past data given by long time frames, rather than concentrating on how the trend may act in the future. Trends do reverse and fluctuate; it is up to the investor to decipher the patterns and make informed decisions on how to act on the trend.

How Realistic Is Getting Rich in Investing?

There are several ways that investors can maximize their investments. Of course, practicing proper business techniques will help you get the most out of it. However, there are several other ways that investors can do this, such as reducing investment costs, increasing diversification, rebalancing, among other techniques. It is important to know all the possible ways to maximize your own investments because you don't know what you don't know. Every bit counts. Just saving a little here and there will add up and your goal will be achieved quickly.

Investors may maximize their investments by decreasing the cost of investing. There are several ways that investing may cost one money, and that money is coming directly out of the investment. Investors may switch from hiring a financial advisor to doing the investing themselves, cutting the costs of the commission. Investors commonly forget about transaction costs. There is typically a flat fee for buying stock through a broker. Instead of making many small purchases, investors may save up and only buy stocks in certain increments (for example, perhaps the investor won't buy more stocks until they have saved $1000). By doing this, a much smaller percentage of the investment is being cut out and used to cover those fees. This may require more patience, but that money will add up. Lowering one's expenses will increase their return. Instead of being spent, that money may be growing and earning a return on it. Because of compound interest, this money will earn money on itself and multiply over the years. This is why it's crucial to save every bit possible.

Investors must also really pay attention to their portfolios. Diversification is crucial, and it can save the investor from losing all of their investment. Markets typically fall much more quickly than markets rise. This means that the investor must prepare for such occurrences. It is important to regularly rebalance one's portfolio to ensure that it is positioned correctly for the investor to make the largest possible gains.

Investors must also truly pay attention to what they want. Maximizing one's investments will depend on the person and what their goals are. Although it is wise to listen to the advice of experts and see what other ways that one may invest, it is crucial to follow the path that is best for the goals and preferences of the individual. This is why a plan is necessary and should be followed. Investors must not stop investing. This is another way to take advantage of compound interest. The investor's portfolio should never stop growing. This growth should be due to both growths in the investment and regular contributions by the investor themselves. Despite the great returns that may be experienced in a bull market, contributions are still necessary. Bear markets should also not discourage investors from continuing investing; this can be a great time to get a good deal on a stock!

How to Be a Winning Trader While Everyone Else Loses

When it comes to trading, there are some important personality traits that you need to possess if you would like to be successful. Not everyone will do well with day trading. It is a fast-paced world of investing, and you can quickly lose a lot of money in the process. And if you do not possess the right characteristics, you will find that you increase your risk of losing money more than before.

Before you decide to get into the world of day trading, you should consider whether you have the right personality to start this field. It can be tough for some people, but with the right personality traits, it will be a great option to help you make some money.

Some of the personality traits that you need to possess to do well with day trading include:

- Personal independence: This is a good work from home business. You need to enjoy the freedom of working on your own and not having someone looking over your shoulders all of the time. If you are not able to motivate yourself to get the work done or you thrive when you are in an office setting, you may find that it is difficult to get started in this kind of business.

- Decisiveness: When you are dealing with the market over the long term, you will notice that the market stays pretty steady. But when you work in the market on one day, there are a lot of ups and downs, and the market may change on you in just a few seconds. Because of this, a day trader needs to be able to make quick and decisive decisions to keep them in the market. As a good day trader, you will need to rely on some of your past experiences to read what is going on with a new situation and make your decisions. There isn't a ton of room for second-guessing when it comes to day trading.

- Discipline and persistence: Since you do not have a boss on your back when you work in day trading, you need to be able to keep yourself focused on the task at hand, to watch the market, do your research, and be prepared to make the right decisions to make more money. And you need to realize that there will be a time when you are learning the ropes, and it may not be going the way that you would like. However, once you find a strategy that works for you and helps you to make a profit, then you will stick with it.

- Interest in trading: Good traders will have some enthusiasm for the market for a long time before deciding to get into day trading. You should already have a natural inclination to follow commodities, bonds, stocks, and some of the other securities that are available. If you do not really have any interest in business or finances at all, then this will be a struggle to become a day trader.

- Personal support: You need to have your own discipline and to be self-motivated, it is still nice to have some personal support throughout the day. The daily life of a day trader can be stressful and having some friends and family who will help you to keep in touch with the world can make a big difference.

- Financial independence: It is not a requirement to have a ton of money to get started with day trading. With that being said, you need to have enough that you can do your chosen trades and then still have a little bit of a safety net in case the trades do not do that much. You should never trade with money that you cannot afford to lose. If you are someone who is living paycheck to paycheck, you need to take some time to build up savings before you even get started with day trading.

- Understand technology: All of your day trading will happen on your computer. If you do not have some familiarity with using a computer and with some of the platforms that are available, you will have a hard time working with day trading.

- Can keep your cool: there will be times, even with a good day trading strategy, when you make the wrong decisions, and your stocks will lose you money. If you are not able to keep your cool, you will end up making the situation a lot worse. You need to be able to look at the situation, whether you are earning or losing money, and make good decisions that will help you to turn things around or to at least limit your losses.

There are a lot of different parts that come with becoming a day trader, and if you are not in the right frame of mind or do not have the personality for this; you will be disappointed with the lack of results that you will get. It takes a specific person to do day trading, and for those who do not have the right personality, it is best to pick out different investing options.

The What, the When, the How

What are you going to trade?

When are you going to make those trades?

How are you going to make money on those trades? Thus, when are you going to get out?

What's your expected risk? When do you reevaluate if things aren't going as planned? How do you test a different approach so that you can find the best way for you to make money in the markets?

What to do if the market gaps up, gaps down, trends up, trends down, or trades sideways and bounces back and forth between the two?

You need to answer all of these questions. You need to examine what you believe in the market and why.

You need to break down each market you're going to trade and explain how you've come to believe what you believe of each of these markets, and what your thoughts are on how to trade them.

Once that's done, you should be ready to start looking at your system as a whole.

Manage Losses

Winners take care of themselves. Losers are the only thing you have to know to manage. When you are trading and you are taking a risk with your money, you need to know when you're getting into a trade and when you're getting out of one.

Most people spend all their time trying to figure out the perfect system to get into winning trades. Most winners spend all their time trying to figure out how to not have a losing trade. There is a difference and a very big difference at that. If you don't think so, you will by the end of this section.

For winning traders, they expect to spend money on trade sometimes, but they never want to lose money. Which is to say, they never want to lose more than they have to on a trade when they are wrong? It is the only time when they lose money. The market moves against them. They get out down 1% of their account, and they're fine. Ready to get back in when the next set-up announces itself. What a winning trader hates is when they abandon their own system, start doubling down on their bet, go on tilt, and suddenly, they are down to 5%, 10%, even 20% of their account, when at 1%, they could have known that they were wrong.

Losing traders think that is a normal process. They have excuses. The market just would not cooperate. The President made a tweet and it sent the markets into chaos; otherwise, I'd have been right. My broker cheats the market to get you kicked out of your position, and then the market turns around and does what it was supposed to do. On and on, it goes. Because, for the losing trader, it's easy to blame everyone and anyone else, except the person whose responsibility it is for them to come home with money each day–themselves!

The market doesn't care about you. It's not waiting for you to make the trade and then go in the exact opposite direction the moment your trade goes in. The market is nothing but an engine to make, lose, and spend money. Which one you do is always up to you?

So, how do you go about managing your losses?

Know Your Stop

Once you have defined your exit, you need to put a stop there, so that you're automatically closed out of the position the moment it goes against you. Why? Because when it's left up to you, that means you can start talking to yourself and saying, "I think I'm right, I'm just going to hold this position." You don't need that stress or that ability to mess yourself up like that. It's stressful when you have to decide whether or not to get out of a trade. It's easy when it's done for you and you can reevaluate the market without the need for it to go the way your position is going.

Traders who trade without a stop order are like people who ride motorcycles without a helmet. It feels good; you think you're safe, you know you're a great driver until your brains are all over the sidewalk. Stop orders make everything easier. And they're the number one tool to profitable traders.

CHAPTER 1:

OPTION BASICS FOR BEGINNERS

What Are Options?

By definition, an option is a financial derivative or contract that allows you to purchase or sell a financial asset within a predetermined cost and time frame. The predetermined date or time frame is also known as the exercise date. For options trading to take place, the seller must meet all the requirements of the trade.

Options trading differs from market to market, and from platform to platform. As a trader, you must be able to differentiate between the various categories of options, including ETF options, stock options, and futures options, among several others.

Options are considered a low-risk form of trade because you can terminate a contract before the exercise or expiry date. The value of an option only represents a percentage of a seller's underlying security or asset.

The price at which the buyer agrees to place for the option is called the strike price, while the fee used to purchase the option contract is called the premium.

How Do Options Work?

When it comes to looking at the worth of options contracts, this is determined by the probability of future price events occurring. If something is more likely to happen, its option will be more expensive.

If the value of a stock is increasing, the cost of the call will increase too. This is a great way to understand how the value of a call works.

If an option has lesser time for it to expire, the lower the value of such an option is. This occurs because the probability of a price moving in that stock reduces as the expiry date draws near. That's one reason an option is said to be a wasting asset.

Let's say you purchase an out of money one-month option, and its stock refuses to increase, the option loses its value as each day goes by.

Time is an important aspect of the option price, meaning that a one-month option will end up being less valuable than a choice of three months. Why this is so is the fact that there is a lot of time, meaning that there is a chance that the price can improve.

The same can be said for an option that expires in a year is more valuable than one that expires in a month even when they are derivatives of the same stock.

The reason it has this characteristic is because of time decay. That option that had a great worth the previous day would have its worth reducing the next day.

Another thing that is said to improve the worth of an option is volatility. This occurs because the uncertainty factor improves the odds of a result occurring. When an asset's volatility level increases, the greater price swings improve the chances of substantial moves going down and up. When you notice more massive price swings, it means that there is a great chance that an event will happen, meaning that the higher the level of volatility, the higher the option's price.

Volatility and Options trading are related to each other.

In a lot of U.S. exchanges, a stock option contract is seen as the alternative to sell or purchase 100 shares. This is one reason a contract premium is multiplied by 100 to have access to the total amount that will be spent to purchase the call.

In a lot of cases, buyers decide to have their profits taken by trading out their position. What this means is that the option holders can decide to sell their options, while the writers purchase their positions again.

The alterations in the prices of options are explained by either extrinsic value or intrinsic value. This is also called time value.

The premium of an option is seen as mixing the time value and intrinsic value. The intrinsic value is that options contract's in-the-money amount. In the case of a call option, this is that amount that is higher than what the stock is currently trading for.

As for the time value, it shows the extra value a trader is expected to spend on an option, which is higher than the intrinsic value. This is what is called the time value or extrinsic value.

What Is an Option Contract?

An option contract is basically an agreement struck connecting two traders to trade an asset at an established date and price. Option contracts are common in the trade of commodities, securities as well as real estate investments.

Normally, an option contract comprises of the following:

The type of Option - This can either be a call or put option. A call option allows you to purchase a specific number of shares over time, while a put option is for buying shares of a certain commodity or security on specified terms.

The Unit of Trade refers to a single indivisible amount of any trade item. For options, the common unit of trade is a contract.

The Strike Price – as stated earlier, this is the price at which an options contract can be exercised (sold or bought). In the case of a call option, it is the cost where the shares are bought by the buyer before the expiration date. For the put option, it refers to the cost at which the shares can be sold by the buyer before the expiration date.

Underlying security is the commodity, bond, index, currency, or stock used to establish the worth of an option. This value is derived from the price or performance of the underlying security.

The expiration date is the last day for buying or selling an option.

Other Types of Options

Besides the call and put options, there are several other types of options you can trade in on the market. These are categorized using the methods used for trade, underlying securities, and the expiration cycle. You, however, have to bear in mind that not all of them are suitable for intraday trading. Some of these options include:

- Index options
- Options on futures
- Stock options
- Weekly SPY options
- Mini and Mini Index options
- ETF options
- IRA Accounts
- QQQ options
- Crude oil options

- OEX options
- ES Weekly options
- ITM options
- E-Mini options
- S & P options

Know the Lingo

When it comes to trading options effectively, one of the first things you are going to want to do is to familiarize yourself with the common terms that options traders are likely to use to ensure that even if you can't trade like a professional at least, you can speak like one.

Strike Price

The price of a given underlying asset at the moment the option is purchased is called its strike price.

Exercised

When the movement of an underlying asset makes the specifications of a given option favorable, then it is exercised or taken advantage of and the ownership of the underlying asset changes hands.

Trade out

If a holder exercises an option that the writer feels is not worth the current market value of the underlying asset, then they can trade out, which means they essentially buy back the holder's shares and relist them because they believe that a better deal is readily available even with the additional trouble taken into account. All told, some 50 percent of trades expire without any action being taken. Of the remaining 50 percent, only 10 percent is actually exercised, with the remaining 40 percent ending up getting traded out.

Listing

The process of creating a new call is referred to as listing an option. Listed options appear on national exchanges, and it is recommended that you only deal with listed options until you make it past your options trader novice phase. If you are dealing with vanilla options, then you can realistically expect all of the options you find to include 100 shares of the underlying stock in question.

In the money

If an option is currently in the money, then the underlying stock that it is tied to is currently sitting at a point that is above whatever it is you initially paid for it. If, however, it is out of the money instead, then this means that it previously was in the money but has now dropped back down to a point where it is no longer profitable.

If the underlying stock is exactly at the price at which you originally purchased it, then the option can currently be thought of as at the money.

Value

The value of the underlying stock related to a given option can be broken into two parts, intrinsic and time. Intrinsic value is the difference between the current price and the strike price, assuming it is a positive difference.

If the difference is negative, then the intrinsic value is said to be zero, as it cannot be a negative number. Time value is simply the amount of time that the option has until it expires, with options with a lower amount of time value having a lower overall value as a result.

Premium

The sum total of the intrinsic value, stock price, time value, strike price and the total amount of volatility is said to be an option's premium.

Understanding Pricing Influences

When it comes to being an effective options trader, one of the most important things that you will learn is how the various types of different options that you see come by the value that they are currently assigned. The price of a specific option is an amalgamation of its volatility, the price of the underlying asset, the amount of interest involved and the intrinsic and time value. As such, when it comes to deciding on which options to pursue, you are going to need to understand the different between what are known as premiums (guaranteed profits) and the theoretical maximum value (what the option should currently be worth based on the visible signs).

Price of the underlying asset

While they often will not move at the same speed or for the same amounts, an option is always going to follow the lead of its underlying asset. As such, you can always expect the price of related calls to increase along with rising asset prices, while puts will always decrease and vice versa.

Intrinsic value

The amount of value that an option is going to hold onto, even at the very end of its lifespan, is known as the intrinsic value. When working with a call option, you can find the intrinsic value by taking the current price of the underlying asset and dividing that by the difference between the strike price and the current price. When it comes to finding the intrinsic value of a put option, the process is mostly the same; to start, you subtract the amount the underlying asset is currently worth from its strike price before dividing that number by the current stock price. The results of this equation will provide you with a clearer idea of the type of advantage that choosing to exercise the option at the moment would provide you with. This number can also be thought of as the minimum that the option will ever be worth, even at the moment of its expiration.

Time value

The amount of time that an option has until it expires is directly related to how likely that same option is going to ultimately end in a profit greater than the intrinsic value before things are said and done. To determine the amount of time value that the option you are considering currently offers you will want to find the current price of the option and subtract from it the amount of intrinsic value that the same option currently has. It is common for options to hold onto 70 percent of their total value, or more, during the first half of their lifetime before losing value much more rapidly after that point. It is also important to note that time value can change dramatically based on the volatility of the underlying asset both in the moment and based on its expectations in the future. As a general rule, the lower the time value, the more stable the option is likely to be.

Volatility

Compared to the other factors that most affect options pricing, volatility is much more subjective, though measuring it properly is still important as well. This can be easier said than done, however, especially for those traders who are still new to the process. Luckily, there are a wide variety of programs that track such things automatically online these days, so the problem is much less pronounced. The historical volatility of a specific option can be found by taking into account the overall volatility of its underlying asset in both the short and the long term. Volatility is especially important to be aware of if you expect a major shakeup in the near future as it will show you how the underlying asset responded the last time events unfolded this way, which makes it more likely that events will repeat themselves next time around.

Why You Should Trade Options

Let us look at some of the most notable reasons why one may need to trade options, besides making serious money.

Low prices

While trading options, you can create and close contracts faster and with minimal risk compared to other securities. The cost of purchasing an option is relatively cheaper than that of buying the underlying security, or shares in the case of stock trading. This means that you can make more profit using less capital.

High possibility of success

It is easier to make a profit from options since you do not need to close a contract to gain from it. Options are also highly volatile.

Diverse markets

There are numerous investment opportunities related to options trading. These opportunities are often cheaper than the purchase of actual stock. The more you increase your capital, the more your profit potential grows.

It can be combined with stock trade

To maximize profits, you can easily combine options with stock trading. Doing this allows you to increase your stock from the profits made in trading options.

Easy to access

Various online platforms give you the opportunity to trade options from all over the world. With some good capital, all you need is a good internet connection to get started.

Disadvantages

Despite the many benefits of options trading, there are a few drawbacks that come with it. However, these are less likely to impact your experience in the trade and can be overlooked. Some disadvantages that come to mind include:

An extensive spread

A bid-ask spread is a variation between the maximum price that the buyer is ready to place and the minimum price the seller is prepared to allow for the asset. The spread is quite wide when selling options as compared to stocks trade. This is due to the reduced liquidity associated with the options markets and has a great impact on the profit of any daily trade.

Reduced price movements

In trading options, the changes in the price are limited to the time value of the contract and premium. Although this value increases with the cost of the underlying instrument, the profit may be reduced significantly in case the time value diminishes.

These drawbacks are highly insignificant and should not prevent you from engaging in the trade of options. You can easily adjust your trading plans to minimize their impact.

Types of Options

The two main types of options are called call options and put options. We will address the specifics of each type below.

Call Options

Most commonly just simply called a call; this type of option allows the trader of the option the right to buy the associated asset on or before the expiration date. The reason that anyone would be interested in buying the attached asset is because the price is expected to rise within the lifetime of the option. As a result, the profit lies in the price of the asset going above the strike price. The seller makes a profit from the trader paying him or her a premium for that option. In the event that the asset does rise in price, then the buyer of the option has the right to exercise the option to buy the asset or sell the option. Both strategies lead to a profit for the buyer. In this scenario, the buyer has the potential for unlimited income, while the seller's income is limited to the premium paid for that option.

The terms that describe whether or not a trader has made a profit include in the money, out of the money and at the money. In the money describes the situation whereby the asset price has gone above the strike price. This is favorable and describes a profitable situation for the trader.

Out of the money describes the situation whereby the asset price has fallen below the strike price resulting in a loss from the option. At the money means that the asset price is equivalent to the strike price and so the trader does not profit or loss from the option.

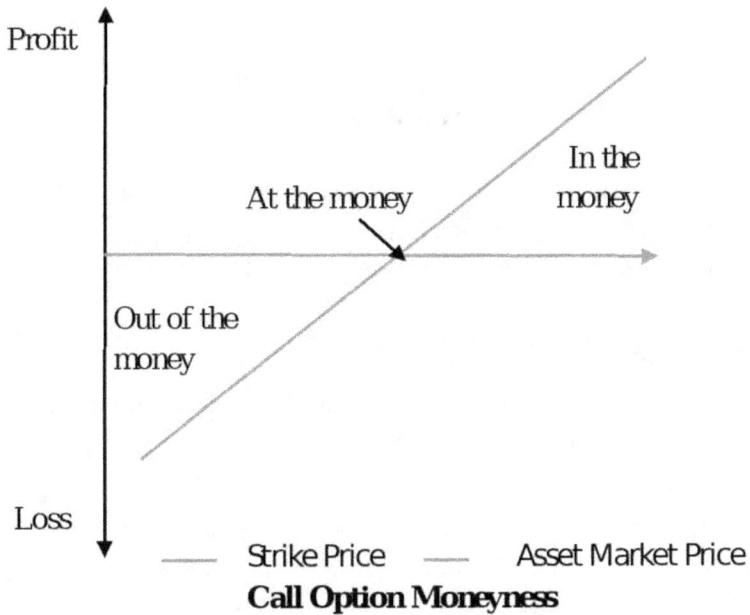

Call Option Moneyness

Put Options

Also commonly called a put, this type of option gives the trader the right to sell the asset attached to the contract at the strike price on or before the expiration date. Just like with a call option, the strike price is predetermined with this type of option.

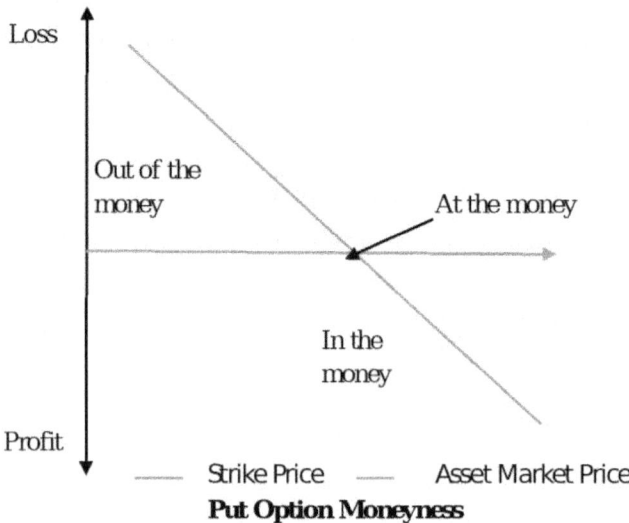

If the trader is in the money by the expiration date, he or she has the option to sell the asset associated with the option by a fixed time or sell the option to someone else.

Going Long vs. Going Short

While they are polar opposites, going long and going short both describe the state of ownership of the asset associated with the option. Going short is also known as having a short position. It describes the state of the seller not owning the asset associated with the option. Going long is also described as having a long position. It means that the seller owns the asset associated with the option.

As you can see, neither of these options refers to the time period associated with that option. Rather, the focus is on the ownership of the associated asset. As such, the person who owns the asset is called the long position holder. If this person expects the price of the asset to rise, then this is called having a bullish view. This applies to a trader holding a long call option.

If this person expects the price of the asset to fall, this is known as having a bearish view. This is the scenario where a trader has a long put option.

Financial Leverage

Leverage is a term that is, in most cases, made use in financial management. It comes up from borrowing capital as a way of funding as well as expanding an investment. It will then generate some returns on the risk capital. It is a strategy to invest in using money that is borrowed. It increases the profits of the investment made. Leverage can as well be the debt amount that a company puts in use to finance its assets. When the leverage is high, that means that the investor has more debt that has accumulated than the equity. Leverage is known to boost the returns and hence, an increase in the profit.

It multiplies the potential returns from a particular investment. It will bring down the likely to come up in case the investment you have made does not turn out as you had expected. The idea of leverage is put I use by investors as well as firms. An investor will use to make sure that there is an increase in returns on the investment. The investment will be levered using specific instruments, including margin accounts, options as well as futures. Companies will use leverage to finance their assets. Instead of issuing stock so that they can raise capital, they decide to use the debt to finance, aiming to increase the shareholder value.

Investors do not prefer to use leverage immediately. They have their means to access it indirectly. They opt to invest in a company that they know uses force to fund as well as expand their investments. The company does not have to increase the outlay necessarily. Leverage is an excellent approach anyone can put in use to multiply the buying power in the trade out there. However, you can decide to use margin as a way of creating leverage.

There are several types of leverage, but they do not need to be combined with being productive. They instead form the entire process even though they are independent. They include;

Operating Leverage

Operating leverage is just concerned with the investment activities of an individual firm. It is about the incurrence of the fixed cost of operation in a company's income stream. The operating price can either be fixed, semi-fixed, variable as well as semi-variable. The fixed fee is contractual, and it is subject to time. It does not necessarily have to change when the sales change, and it is supposed to be paid despite the number of sales. Variable cost t has a direct variation in the level of sales revenue. There will be no variable cost if there will be no any sales that are made in a certain period. Semi-variable, as well as semi-fixed, will vary partly with the number of purchases made, and it will remain partially fixed. The fixed operating cost can be subject to be put in a lever, and hence the decisions of investment will go in favor of using assets that have a fixed price. When a firm decides to use the fixed cost, it will increase the effect that a change will have on the sales when EBIT changes. The ability that a firm will have to put the fixed operating cost in use to increase its earnings before the interest, as well as the taxes, is what is known as operating leverage. The leverage will be concerning the variation of the sales as well as profit. When the percentage of the operating cost is high, and then there will be a rise in the level of operating cost.

Financial Leverage

When there are financial charges in existence, the financial leverage will as well exist. The business costs should not depend on the operating profits in any way. The sources in which the funds that help to boost an investment come from can be put in categories. The funds can either be having a fixed charge, and some may not be having the fixed financial cost. Debentures, preference shares, bonds as well as long-term loans have a fixed financial burden. Equity shares are known to have no fixed charge at all.

The fixed financial charge is used as a lever, and hence, the business decisions will go in favor when you employ such funds. When there are fixed charges in a company's income stream, financial leverage will be an outcome.

It is an excellent idea to make sure that the change that will be made in EBIT to affect EPS will be significant. The higher the level of fixed charges, the higher the probability that the degree of financial leverage will go up. When the fixed costs do down, the economic advantage will go down as well.

Combined Leverage

If you bring both the operating leverage and the financial leverage together, they will come up with the combined force. It is concerning the risk of one not being able to cover up for the total amount of the fixed charges when a firm can cover fully on the operating as well as the financial burdens, that is when the term combined leverage comes in. The higher the fixed operating cost as well as the financial charges, the higher the level of the combined force.

Working Capital Leverage

When there is a decrease in the investment of a particular asset, there will be an increase in profit. That means that risks, as well as returns, have direct relations.

When the probability of risk goes up, there is a likely hood that the profit will increase as well. The ability of an individual firm to increase the effect of the change in the current stock on the firm's returns is working capital leverage. It is so when there is an assumption that the liabilities are constant.

How to Start Trading Options

Trading options is straightforward. Beginners can join the team of traders in a few steps as highlighted below:

Create a Brokerage Account

You need this account to liaise with your traders easily. Since options trading has become so much popular, the internet has a good number of brokers to select from. You must, however, ensure that you get one that suits your trading needs. When selecting an online broker, put the following factors into consideration.

Carry out some research on different brokers and compare their charges in terms of commission. This will ensure that you get the best competitive spreads. Be sure to check out whether there are hidden charges as well.

Develop a Strategy

Once you are done creating a brokerage account, you will need to create a winning strategy. Options trading strategies come in various designs. Some are straightforward, while others need a lot of time and resources. A good strategy is one that has several components in it. These include

Charts and patterns

Charts and patterns are a must for each trading engagement. They help you study and easily understand the history of an option. Each chart must have a good indicator for trading options. These indicators vary for each strategy and may include the Money Flow Index, Relative Strength Index, Bollinger Bands, Open Interest, and the Put-Call Ratio Indicator. You need more time to understand and practice pattern trading with options. However, you will need to try out a number of charts until you get one that is straightforward and easy to understand.

Timing

When it comes to trading options, time is of the essence. You must understand when to set up a trade, enter into contracts and when to make an exit. For a strategy to work there must be a trader who is willing to place contracts early enough. For instance, you may need to start as early as 6:00 am if you want to get the direction of the day's trade early enough.

Once you have determined the day's trend, you can use the information to come up with a strategy depending on how the market has been at night. You can take the E-mini option, for example, since up to 70% of stocks are entitled to move in the same direction during the day. It is good to note that the U.S stock market dictates the direction of trade in other countries. So, it is important to give the market an hour every morning for it to stabilize before sealing any contracts for the day

In and Out of the Money

The terms "in the money" and "out of the money" are slang used by options traders to indicate whether an option is really worth something or not. It turns out that even out of the money options are worth something, but before we get to that, let's learn what these terms mean and how different call options fit in with the definitions.

The first definition you need to know about is "in the money." A call option is in the money when the strike price of the call option is lower than the current share price. In other words, a call option is in the money when you can buy the shares at a discount price relative to the market price.

To really be worth it, however, you need to understand how the breakeven price fits in. If the stock is trading at $101 a share, technically speaking a call option with a strike price of $100 a share is in the money. However, if you paid $2 per share for that option, then it is not really in the money, because you'd lose $1 a share exercising the option.

So from a practical standpoint, an option has to be positioned such that the market share price has raised enough to account not only for the strike price, but also the price paid to buy the call option. So you need to pay more attention to the breakeven price rather than the in the money price – if you are interested in buying the shares of stock.

When Is an Option Liquid?

Liquidity is one of the most important concepts in finance and trading. Simply put, liquidity is a measure (vague, but real) of how quickly you can convert something into cash.

A cashier's check is very liquid. Cash is 100% liquid. A bar of gold is pretty liquid because you can take it to a gold or coin dealer and sell it immediately for cash. Stocks are liquid, but less liquid than these items because you can't immediately access the cash you get from selling stocks (most brokers will make you wait a few days).

You can compare liquidity between different types of assets. To explain what we mean, let's focus only on options. Some options are going to be more liquid than others. No matter what, your broker is going to have rules on being able to get the cash-out, but that isn't our concern when talking about the liquidity of options. Those rules are going to apply to all options.

Our concern here is how easy it is to buy and sell a particular option.

Options trading can move fast. In my own experience, I have seen options that I've purchased lose and gain $100 or more over a matter of 30-90 minutes. The rapid price movements of options coupled with the fact that they lose value through time decay every single day that passes means that when the time is right to get in and out of an options contract, you want to be able to do it right away.

So the concept of liquidity when it comes to trading options comes down to being able to buy and sell an option instantly. The market provides two important pieces of information that you can use in order to determine how liquid an option is.

Leverage and Options Trading

The reason why trading options strategy is so profitable compared to that of other securities is due to leverage. A small amount of money can leverage larger underlying security compared to the same amount placed in stocks or bonds, for instance.

With $100, you can probably buy 20 shares valued at $5 per share. However, this same amount of money can probably control 100 shares. This is what leverage is. When it comes to profits, the options trader will make a much larger profit compared to the stock trader. If you have trading capital, then you can make a much higher profit if you choose to trade options rather than stocks or any other security. The potential is huge and ranges in the 1000% possibility.

Options leverage is defined as the money equivalent in multiples of a single option position about the true cash value of an underlying asset. When these two are compared, then the difference becomes visibly noticeable. This is why options are considered so valuable. The potential they hold is astronomical.

Buying and Selling Options

If an options contract is "in the money," this means that the option can be exercised by a buyer to earn a profit, which means either buying or selling 100 shares of stock. On the other hand, if it is "out of the money," then it would not be profitable for the buyer to exercise the option. Sellers of options contracts generally hope that the option will be out of the money. If a contract was to expire and it was out of the money, it is said to "expire worthless." Since the contract has expired without any value, the seller of the option pockets any money they received selling it, and they don't have to worry about buying or selling shares of stock.

A buyer of an option is normally a trader. That means they are hoping to sell it at a higher price than they paid for it. As the price of the stock goes up and down, it can cause the market price of any options contract on that stock to move up or down. This provides traders with an opportunity to earn profits without actually investing in the stock. When the value of an option goes up, they can sell the option to another trader for a profit.

Keep in mind that if you buy an option to enter your investment position, you are not under any sort of obligation. In other words, if you later sell the option, you are not under the seller's obligation. Only the original seller of an option is required to either buy or sell shares of stock. So, you can buy an option, and if its value goes up, you can sell it off and take a profit and walk away from it. Many people trade options without having any intention to own the shares of stock or trade shares of stock whatsoever. But if you want to, you can definitely buy or sell the shares if it becomes advantageous and you can afford it.

CHAPTER 2:

TRADING FUNDAMENTALS

Before you setup your options day trading business, there are a few things you need to have intimate knowledge of. They are your current financial circumstances, the time you are able to commit to day trading and your risk profile. Create a financial balance sheet that lists your expenses, and any other income that you obtain. This will allow you to assess your financial health and how much you can invest into options. This also allows you to know what risks you can take while trading options. Never invest capital or resources that you cannot afford to lose and never trade beyond your trading experience level. Becoming an options day trader requires a healthy time investment at the beginning because you need to learn your way around this arena as well as set up a strong foundation for your profile. Do not rush and squander your money in an overzealous move to get started.

Next, before you risk your hard-earned money, learn to trade options on paper. This is called paper trading and allows you to use real-life scenarios to assess your performance when it comes to trading options.

When you are ready to move forward to real-time practice, find a brokerage firm to represent you. Online brokerage firms are growing in popularity, but ensure that you properly research the firm to ensure reputability and that you are paying as little in commissions as possible. You may even be able to find a broken that does not charge commissions.

The brokerage firm will help you get set up as a qualified options trader at the level that is relevant for your experience as well as aid in setting up the appropriate accounts. You need to be able to process payments and other financial transfers online before you approach a broker.

Lastly, ensure that you have the tools for the trade. Ensure that your internet connection is fast and reliable. Also, ensure that your computer or laptop has a fast processor and adequate memory to prevent crashes as trading programs rely on a fast-moving computer. Most traders have a need for at least 2 monitors to keep abreast as to what is happing on the financial market.

Entry into the Options Trading Market

There are several different types of options that a day trader can pursue, but it makes no sense to try to pursue all of them as this will stretch you and your resources thin. The best thing to do is pinned down one or two niches that you will pursue at the beginning to find the ones that fit best with you and your trading style. Popular niches that day traders pursue include stocks, foreign exchange, and exchange-traded funds.

Planning for Success

Options day trading is a business. You need to treat it as such. You will not wake up one day and just start any other type of business with no plan. Therefore, you need to approach day trading options with the same foresight and planning. Just as you would create a business plan for any other type of business, you need to create a trading plan. This will serve as your guide with step-by-step details on how you will approach day trading options, how you will measure your success and how you will grow your business and income. As a result, here are a few vital categories that need to be developed in your trading plan:

Your Goals

Goal setting is a necessary life skill that everyone needs to learn and it will serve you well in this area. These need to be both long-term and short-term. You need to be very specific. Vague notions like "I want to be as successful as I can be," have no place in your trading plan. Your goals need to be quantifiable and trackable.

Setting your goals also allows you to outline what areas you need to improve your knowledge so that you become a better options day trader. You need to develop a system for rewarding yourself when you hit milestones on your goal's list.

An Efficient Workspace

You need to develop a plan for where you will work as well as the equipment that you will need. This does not have to be fancy. All you need is an adequate internet connection, a computer setup, and a working filing system. Ensure that you have plans to upgrade your equipment as needed.

Developing a Time Schedule

It is important to set regular trading hours to ensure that you do not become burnt out and that you maintain your perspective of your career and life. All work and no play leads to sickness. While you are setting working hours, also allocate time off, vacation and sick leave. Working yourself to the bone will remove the sense of fulfillment that you will find with this job. Therefore, finding balance is vital.

Personal Development

As you are your business, you need to ensure that you invest in yourself so that you continuously expand your knowledge of trading and develop yourself as an individual—schedule time for further reading, seminars and other learning tools.

Your trading plan is not set in stone. In fact, it is something that you should continuously evaluate and revise based on the conditions and circumstances that you experience as an options day trader. At the very least, your options trading plan should be re-evaluated once yearly.

Technical Indicators You Need to Know About

When it comes to technical indicators for trading options, there are three indicators that you need to know about to help you make your trades. These indicators are used to help you identify stock trends and patterns so that you can get a strong understanding as to what the stocks are doing and where your best positions are going to be.

You should always check technical indicators as a part of your technical analysis to ensure that the position you are taking is going to earn you the best income possible.

The three technical indicators that you need to know about include the relative strength index indicator (RSI), the moving average convergence divergence indicator (MACD), and the stochastic indicator. Each of these will let you know what is going on with any particular stock and whether or not that stock offers a good position for you to trade-in.

Relative Strength Index (RSI)

The relative strength index is a momentum indicator that sits on a separate scale from the candlestick chart that you will be looking at when you look at the stock market for any given stock value.

The indicator is shown as a single line that is scaled from 0 to 100 and it identifies any stocks that have been overbought or oversold, meaning that you will identify which stocks are due for a rebound in the coming days.

On the indicator, which is shown on the side of the screen, you will notice that there are two white "frames" on either side of it, each of which shows where the market is peaking at overbought or oversold. The top frame represents stocks that have risen over 70 on the indicator, which indicates the market has been overbought and people are about to start selling their shares in order to earn profits before the market switches in the opposite direction.

The bottom frame represents stocks that have dropped below 30 on the indicator, indicating that the market has been oversold and people are about to start buying those stocks. You can watch for trends in any given stock on the RSI to see how they tend to perform and where they are presently sitting based on the intensity of trades that have been happening with that particular stock.

Most stocks will not consistently swing back and forth between overbought and oversold, but instead will straddle one side of the indicator before taking a large swing in the opposite direction at any given point in the future.

With that being said, you should always take your time spotting trends on this indicator so that you can confirm the trend is actually happening. Although this will eat into some of your profits, it will still help you ensure that you are earning plenty from the trade that you are seeking to make.

Moving Average Convergence Divergence (MACD)

The MACD indicator shows a fast line, a slow line, and a histogram that is used to help identify what is taking place with any given stock. This particular indicator can be more challenging to understand, but it still offers a wealth of valuable knowledge that will help you identify how the stock is behaving.

You should take your time to understand the MACD and educate yourself by watching it on the active stock market screen so that you can get a feel for the information it provides you with. Once you understand how to read this indicator, you will find a great deal of information that helps reinforce your trade decisions going forward.

The MACD indicator shows the moving average of the "difference" between the fast line and the slow line on the indicator itself. This means that what you are reading is how quickly the market is moving back and forth, or how volatile the market is with any given stock at any given moment.

The MACD slow line actually shows you the moving average of the last line over a number of periods defined as "MA-periods."

The MACD indicator is shown by two lines with the last line being represented by the color blue and the slow line being represented by the color orange. The bigger the gap is between the two lines, the more volatile the market is. When the two lines cross, it shows that the market has switched in trend, resulting in it either turning bullish or bearish from a bearish or bullish trend, depending on what direction it moves into.

The histogram shows you the moving average of the stock so that you can get a feel for how volatile the stock has been in the past, allowing you to understand whether or not the current volatility of the stock is standard or unusual for that particular stock. If it is standard, you know that the patterns of the stock will more than likely follow patterns similar to the ones it has in the past.

In other words, this is considered a lower risk stock investment. If the indicator suggests that the stock is more volatile, this means that it is less likely to follow historical patterns and that it will likely perform in a more unpredictable manner.

In other words, the stock is riskier and could come with greater losses. With that being said, higher-risk stocks do generally offer higher rewards; too, meaning it may be worth the risk depending on how confident you are in your judgment of how the stock will truly behave.

In essence, a moving average works like any other average. It is the average of the high and low price of an asset over a given period of time.

The average price of an asset over a given period of time is a static measure that simply reflects the buy and sell price of the asset in a rather specific window of time. It is a snapshot, if you will, of what that asset's price has been over a longer period of time.

As such, a moving average becomes the calculation of the average price of an asset at given intervals, for instance, every hour. With this calculation on a recurring basis, the asset's price can be tracked to determine where the trend, if any, lies.

The various results of the moving average calculation can be plotted on a chart in which each point can be used to determine the overall trend of the asset's price. There are three possible types of trends:

Upward Trend

This type of trend indicates that the overall trend in the price of an asset is up, meaning, increase. It is very important to keep in mind that an upward trend is generally accompanied by higher demand though it is not always the case. Nevertheless, increased demand generally means an increase in price.

Downward Trend

This type of trend indicates that the overall trend in the price of an asset down, meaning a decrease. What this indicates is that the price is going down as a result of an increase of supply, or a decrease in demand. Both forces can converge, thus leading the asset's prices to spiral downward.

Sideways Trend

In this case, there is little to no change in the price of the asset. This means that the trend remains steady. When this happens, it is because investors are being cautious. Perhaps they are expecting a breakout. So, while the breakout happens, they are holding their positions in order to see that will transpire.

Additionally, moving averages use a statistical technique called "candlesticks" to track the high and low price of the asset at every interval the price is measured. In this regard, you can visualize the amount of volatility as reflected in the fluctuations of the asset's price. Consequently, you can gain a great deal of perspective as to what the sentiment of investors is with regard to the asset in question.

The main function of a moving average is to track the trend in the price of an asset.

It is the premier tool used by traders and analysts in order to gauge the sentiment of investors. If investors are piling on to an asset, you will see this reflected in the price of the asset. On the contrary, if investors are looking to dump an asset, the moving average will reflect this sentiment.

This is why you, as a day trader, need to recognize these trends. The most important thing to keep in mind is that depending on your overall trading approach, you will be able to figure out what the best play for you is.

Given the fact that the moving average reflects very short-term moves, in addition to longer-term moves, you can figure out if the asset in question is good for a short-term trade, or perhaps it might be better suited for a long-term approach.

Moving averages, when available, can serve to view the price of stocks over a very long period of time, such as several years. This is a powerful analytics tool as you can see what the performance of the stock has been over a much more extended period of time. Consequently, you can choose to hold on to it as part of a passive income strategy or as a means of hedging your portfolio against riskier propositions.

So, I would greatly encourage you to become familiar with moving averages as this will be the basic parameter by which you will be able to measure the performance of stocks, and any other asset, you wish to trade.

Stochastic Indicator

The stochastic indicator is a momentum indicator that can help you identify when a trend might end, letting you know when a stock has either been overbought or oversold. The information given by the stochastic indicator is similar to what you receive from an RSI, meaning that it can help validate whether or not the trade position you are looking at is ideal.

The stochastic indicator is shown by two lines on a chart that is separate from the candlestick chart that represents the market itself. Typically, it is shown below the market chart and follows the exact same time stamps, meaning that the information you see in the stochastic indicator chart perfectly overlaps with the information you see in the market itself.

The stochastic indicator looks almost exactly like the RSI, with a frame on each the top and bottom of the chart itself, showing you the overbought and oversold portions of the market, respectively.

However, the stochastic indicator has two lines, a red and a blue line, moving through the chart to give you information about what is currently going on in the marketplace.

When the lines are above the "80" point, this means a downtrend is likely to follow, or the market is likely to go bearish. In this case, you would want to sell your call options or buy your put options, depending on what strategy you are using to earn your profits from the market.

If it drops below the "20" point, the market has been oversold and it is going to turn into an uptrend or a bullish market. This is where you would want to buy your call options, sell your put options, or otherwise position yourself with the best spread and strategy to earn profits from the incoming movement of the stock prices.

When reading the stochastic indicator, you want to see **both** lines rise above 80 or fall below 20 to indicate that there is a strong chance for the market to switch directions. If only one line crosses, this suggests that the market may be reaching overbought or oversold, but it has not reached it yet and therefore, it is not yet ready to swing back in the opposite direction.

Pay close attention to these stocks; however, as they will likely mature into their overbought or oversold position quickly, leading to an opportunity for you to secure an entry into the market.

Technical Analysis for Evaluating a Trade

Options trading requires less technical analysis than other trade styles, but you are still required to perform technical analysis to ensure that the market entry point you are looking at is going to be profitable. Entering any market at any time without having first completed proper technical analysis can lead to a greater risk of losses due to not clearly understanding what is likely going to happen with the market in its current state.

When you perform technical analysis, your goal is to identify possible positions that you can enter, validate the quality of those positions, choose the position(s) you will take, and then pick the perfect entry point. By following this exact system for entering the market, you can feel confident that you are entering the market at the best possible time, every single time. This way, you maximize your potential for profits and minimize your potential for losses.

Remember, the more educated you are on what you are doing and what position you are taking, the more likely you are going to be able to increase your profits with trading.

Conducting technical analysis for options trading should be completed as a routine every time you do it to ensure that you never miss out on a step. This way, you create a strong system that works for validating your positions, and you can always feel confident that you are taking on the best positions possible.

Creating Your Watch List for Possible Positions

The first thing you need to do when you are engaging in technical analysis is to create a watchlist that is complete with possible trade positions that you can take on that day. You can start identifying possible positions by looking at various stock news sites like the ones I mentioned earlier in this book to help you get a feel for what is going on in the market.

Using these news sites to identify possible positions simply helps by giving you the opportunity to narrow down your scope so that you are only looking at a few places in the market, rather than looking blankly at the market as a whole. This way, you are not spending hours every day scouring for the best possible places.

After you have gauged the market by looking at the news, you can start looking at the market itself to see which positions are looking most favorable. At this point, you can narrow down your listen even further just by getting a simple once over at the market itself. This should help you identify 3-5 positions, or possibly a few more, that may be ideal for you to take on for the day. If you have more than 3-5, start by picking the 3-5 that are most likely to be profitable and conduct your research on these positions, first.

It is likely that you will find your best positions this way, however, if for some reason none of the ones you have looked at seem good, you can move on to the next 3-5 options to find a better position.

Validating the Quality of Your Possible Positions

Now that you have located a few possible positions that you could trade-in, you need to start the process of validating which ones are truly going to be a good position for you to hold and which ones are not.

You can find that out by conducting a deeper background analysis on the stocks through looking at the technical analysis indicators we talked about in the last section, as well as doing a deeper dive on any news relating to that stock.

If you are looking at a good position, everything you find out during the research phase should confirm what you already anticipated when you began to look into the position. If the information differs, this does not necessarily mean that it is a bad position, however, it does mean that you are going to have to consider the numbers to decide whether or not it has the capacity to earn you as many profits as you desire.

You also need to decide whether or not you are willing to endure the risk that is being

Choosing Which Position Will Earn Maximum Gains (And Minimize Losses)

Now that you have thoroughly researched how each position is likely to play out and what types of profits you are likely to incur with each one, as well as what risks you are exposed to, you can move into deciding what position you want to take on. Deciding what position, you are going to trade in the market is not entirely a science, although there are some things you are going to want to weigh into your consideration to help you make the best decision.

Picking Your Exact Entry Point

The last part of your analysis comes from deciding when your entry point is going to be. At this point, you have already designed your exit strategy during your research phase, so now you have to decide on when you are going to enter that position in order to maximize your gains.

This part cannot be broken down to a science, either, as there is never a way to truly guarantee what the market is going to do or when it is going to do it. Even if you are confident that the market is about to behave in a certain way, you cannot confidently guarantee the exact moment at which that shift is going to happen. For that reason, you truly just need to pay attention to your indicators, follow the pattern, and make your best-educated guess on when the best timing is for you to enter into a new options trader.

Candlestick Charts and Patterns

Candlestick charts weren't known in the West before the 1980s when they were introduced. However, Japan used this method for centuries, which at the same time makes Japan the place of origin of the candlestick method. As we have already seen before, these charts show the same information as the bar chart that was used in our country's way before we started using the Japanese system. The reason that the candlestick charts became so popular in such a short amount of time is the fact that it is easier to understand, and it uses simple yet innovative body illustration that helps the investor seeing every change at a glance.

Let's recap some of the basic characteristics of the candlestick as the general pattern. Firstly, the total length of the candle represents the trading range for the predetermined period. The body of the candle is connected to the distance between the prices known as the closing price and the opening price. The difference in color shows if the price went up or down for a certain period. The length of the candle also portrays the volatility of the price and the sum of the candle and the "body" of the candle can be viewed as the progress that was made for one day. If the chart shows that the candle's "body" is short, it means that the closing and the opening prices were close or similar. If that is the case, we can say that the buyers and the sellers were in balance.

When it comes to the candlestick chart, we can say that there are regular candles and then that there is Doji. Doji is a special candle which body is just a horizontal line. This line represents closing prices and opening prices, which in case you have Doji are equivalent.

If the candles have long bodies, which will indicate that the trend of the price is strong. If your chart has candles without any wicks, it means that you got Marubozu. Marumboza is an indicator that shows that the trades were only made in the range of the opening and closing prices, thus no trade was made outside of that range. This is a very strong indication, which means that the market was strongly pushing the price only in one direction.

Hammer

When it comes to ideal signals, in Hammer, that signal is represented with a small body. Its wick should be two times longer than the body regardless of the day being up or down for the price trend. Hammer sometimes signals that the trend of the price will reverse. The way to confirm such an assumption and make it actionable is to wait for the following day and see if the price is going to increase. If the price starts rising, it means that your interpretation of trend reversal has been confirmed. This pattern works because of many traders panic, and if the price is down for some time, they will sell at any price. If we try to express this situation in the candle chart, it means that the wick will be pushed down. However, smart investors come in, and they buy, which pushes the price up once again. These trend reversals can last through the whole day and even keep up happening the following day too.

Hanging Man

The Hanging Man is a pattern that looks the same as the Hammer; the only difference is that it comes in an uptrend. Just like before, we search for a change in the price trend on the following day so we could confirm our estimation of the trend's reversal. The psychology, in this case, is that traders mostly decide to take profits. That way, they push the prices down. Still, some of those who are new on the market see this as their chance to buy. That way, they push the price back up. In any case, this candle is considered to be weak. As a reflection of this pattern, it appears that traders have a hunch that this means that the trend is over, so the selling starts to rise again in the following few days.

Inverted Hammer

Once you see the diagrams for the first two candlestick patterns, you will realize that the inverted hammer also has similar characteristics. There is also certain psychology behind its signaling, and we will briefly explain it: Once the downtrend starts weakening and several traders have second thoughts, they start buying in which pushes the prices up. Sellers also come back in the game, which means that the price will close down. However, if the price starts increasing during the following day, than the conclusion is that the weakness of the trend made buyers buying even more while pushing up the prices, and that way, the uptrend started.

Shooting Star

Last but not least, in the set of four related candle signals is the pattern known as the Shooting Star comes, which comes in an uptrend. Everybody knows that beginners or novices if you prefer, tend to buy on the top. Shooting star demonstrates simply the exuberance that the future causes the traders to see the high wick that appears when novices enter the market. The traders who notice this are usually those who appeared thinking that it is time to sell. Just like in every other pattern above, the only way to confirm this is to wait up the following day and to determine if that was the signal that shows that the trend will reverse.

Bullish Engulfing

This is a pattern that consists of two candles, and it is graded as highly probable. When in a downtrend, the first candle pressures that the selling continues. The pressure is strong enough to allow the following candle to open up at an even lower price. But those investors who are smart see an opportunity here, and they start buying on the second candle in this case. This makes the price to grow and launches it above the limit of the preceding period. This is one of the numerous proofs that the real power is in the hands of the buyers and that there is a high possibility that the trend will reverse.

Bearish Engulfing

It has the same concept as bullish engulfing. The thing is that sometimes uptrend can stretch so badly that the opening price can even go higher than the current price in the earlier candle. Smart and experienced investors usually decide to sell on these occasions. The length of the candle, in this case, shows that the trend can be reversed from an uptrend to a downtrend due to the weight of an opinion. Piercing Candle is a pattern that represents a strong bearish candle that is in a downtrend. This candle with another following candle, opens up at a price that is lower than the current one. However, the candle is rallying to have the finishing price, which has the same trading range as the earlier day. This pattern can be seen as a signal for the trend reversal and the reason for that is piercing candle as an indicator that sellers are feeling hopeless. When the low prices go even lower, it is an opportunity for those who consider themselves to be smart investors to start buying and to push prices strongly up. Dark Cloud Cover is a pattern that has entirely the same characteristic as the piercing candle pattern. The only difference is that the dark cloud cover is in an uptrend.

Bullish Harami

This pattern has a name that originated from the Japanese word Harami that means "pregnant." As the name suggests, the reason for this is that according to them, these candlestick patterns have a resemblance to the pregnant women. If you happen to encounter the bullish harami, it means that the market had a lot of active sellers. However, the other candle indicates that the current price became higher. If the second candle finishes up and provides buying enough pressure, you can see it as a signal that there is going to be a change in the price trend. As usual, the following day is a confirmation checker.

Bearish Harami

When a pattern reaches an end of an uptrend, there can be a candle that demonstrates exuberance that some might see as naïve. When the other period opens up, and the price is lower, continuing to go lower as the day goes by, we can say that it indicates second thoughts in buyers. The most probable income of this situation is that the selling will continue regularly and that everything will be resolved once when the price goes into a downtrend.

Keep in mind that trading should never be done based on one strategy or just one resource, which is why we wouldn't recommend that you start trading relying only on the information you gather through the candlestick principle, for example. Remember, the validity of the pattern depends on the right trend in which the pattern needs to work in. Also, many other indicators have to be taken into consideration.

Rules for Successful Trading

Ensuring dependable profits in the financial markets is much more difficult than it seems at first glance. It is assessed that over 75% of all members in the end wash out and take up more secure side interests.

Be that as it may, the financier business once in a while distributes customer disappointment rates, since they're concerned reality may drive away new records, so the washout rate could be a lot higher.

Disregard the Holy Grail

Losing brokers fantasize about the mystery recipe that will mysteriously improve their outcomes. As a general rule, there are no mysteries in light of the fact that the way to progress consistently goes through cautious decision, viable risk the executives, and gifted benefit taking.

Have Realistic Expectations

It is sad to say that many people who enter the options trading industry are doing so to make a quick buck. Options trading is not a get-rich-quick scheme. It is a reputable career that has made many people rich, but that is only because these people have put in the time, effort, study, and dedication to learning the craft and mastering it.

Start Small to Grow a Big Portfolio

Caution is the name of the game when you just get started with day trading options. Remember that you are still learning options trading and developing an understanding of the financial market. Do not jump the gun even if you are eager. After you have practiced paper trading, start with smaller options positions, and steadily grow your standing as you get a lay of the options day trading land. This strategy allows you to keep your losses to a minimum and to develop a systematic way of entering positions.

Know Your Limits

You may be tempted to trade as much as possible to develop a winning monthly average, but that strategy will have the opposite effect and land you with a losing average. Remember that every options trader needs careful consideration before that contract is set up. Never overtrade and tie up your investment fund.

Be Mentally, Physically and Emotionally Prepared Every Day

This is a mentally, physically, and emotionally tasking career, and you need to be able to meet the demands of this career. That means keeping your body, mind and heart in good health at all times. Ensure that you schedule a time for self-care every day. That can be as simple as taking the time to read for recreation to having an elaborate self-care routine carved out in the evenings.

Not keeping your mind, heart and head in optimum health means that they are more likely to fail you. Signs that you need to buckle up and care for yourself more diligently include being constantly tired, being short-tempered, feeling preoccupied and being easily distracted.

To ensure you perform your best every day, here a few tasks that you need to perform:

- Get the recommended amount of sleep daily. This is between 7 and 9 hours for an adult.

- Practice a balanced diet. The brain and body need adequate nutrition to work their best. Include fruits, complex carbs and veggies in this diet and reduce the consumption of processed foods.

- Exercise regularly. Being inactive increases your risk of developing chronic diseases like heart disease, certain cancers and other terrible health consequences. Adding just a few minutes of exercise to your daily routine not only reduces those risks but also allows your brain to function better, which is a huge advantage for an options day trader.

- Drink alcohol in moderation or not at all.

- Stop smoking.
- Reduce stress contributors in your environment.

Do Your Homework Daily

Get up early and study the financial environment before the market opens and look at the news. This allows you to develop a daily options trading plan. The process of analyzing the financial climate before the market opens is called pre-market preparation. It is a necessary task that needs to be performed every day to asset competition and to align your overall strategy with the short-term conditions of that day.

An easy way to do this is to develop a pre-market checklist. An example of a pre-market checklist includes but is not limited to:

- Checking the individual markets that you frequently trade options in or plan to trade options in to evaluate support and resistance.
- Checking the news to assess whether events that could affect the market developed overnight.
- Assessing what other options traders are doing to determined volume and competition.
- Determining what safe exits for losing positions are.
- Considering the seasonality of certain markets are some as affected by the day of the week, the month of the year, *etc.*

Analyze Your Daily Performance

To determine if the options day trading style and strategies that you have adopted are working for you, you need to track your performance. At the most basic, this needs to be done on a daily basis by virtue of the fact that you are trading options daily. This will allow you to notice patterns in your profit and loss. This can lead to you determining the why and how of these gains and losses. These determinations lead to fine-tuning your daily processes for maximum returns. These daily performance reviews allow you to also make determinations on the long-term activity of your options day trading career.

Do Not Be Greedy

If you are fortunate enough to make a 100% return on your investment, do not be greedy and try to reap more benefit from the position. You might have the position turn on you and you can lose everything. When and if such a rare circumstance happens to you, sell your position and take the profits.

Pay Attention to Volatility

Volatility speaks to how likely a price change will occur over a specific amount of time on the financial market. Volatility can work for an options day trader or against the options day trader. It all depends on what the options day trader is trying to accomplish and what his or her current position is.

Use the Greeks

Greeks are a collection of measures that provide a gage of an option's price sensitivity in relation to other factors. Each Greek is represented by a letter from the Greek alphabet. These Greeks use complex formulas to be determined, but they are the system that option pricing is based on. Even though these calculations can be complex, they can be done quickly and efficiently so that options day traders can use them as a method of advancing their trades for the most profitable position.

The 5 Greeks that are used in options trading are:

Delta

This Greek defines the price relationship between an option and its associated asset. Delta is a direct translation of a change in the price of the associated asset into the changing of the price of an option. Call options deltas range from 1 to 0 while put options deltas range from 0 to -1. An example of delta as it relates to a call option is a call option with a delta of 0.5. If the price of the associated asset increases by $200, then the price of the call option will increase by $100.

Vega

This Greek is a measure of the sensitivity of the price of an option to the implied volatility of the associated asset. Option prices are greatly impacted by the volatility of the associated asset's prices because greater volatility translates in a higher chance that the price of the associated asset will reach or surpass the strike price on or before the expiration date of the option.

Theta

This Greek is a measure of the sensitivity of the price of an option to time decay of the value of the option. Time decay describes the rate of deterioration in the value of the contract because of the passage of time.

The closer the expiration date becomes, the more time decay accelerates because the time left to gain a profit narrows. Therefore, the longer it takes to reach an options' expiration date, the more value this option has because it has a longer time period to gain the trader a profit. The theta is a negative figure because time is always a diminishing factor. This figure becomes increasingly negative the closer the expiration date becomes.

Gamma

This Greek measures the rate of change of the delta of an option. At its most basic, it tells the likelihood of an option reaching or surpassing the strike price.

Rho

This Greek is a measure of an option's value compared to changes in interest rate. Options with longer expiration dates are more likely to be affected by changes in interest rates.

Be Flexible

Many options day traders find it difficult to try trading styles and strategies that they are not familiar with. While the saying of, "Do not fix it if it is not broken," is quite true, you will never become more effective and efficient in this career if you do not step out of your comfort zone at least once in a while. Yes, stick with want work but allow room for the consideration that there may be better alternatives.

Have an Accountability Partner or Mentorship?

Day trading options can be a rather solitary career. That means it becomes easy to sleep in if the urge strikes or just not put in a day of work. While there is nothing wrong with doing that when you have established a solid career in day trading options, this is a slippery slope that can become a harmful habit to your career. Having an accountability partner is an easy way to keep you on track with your trading plan and goals. It keeps you consistent with your actions. This can be a fellow trader, your spouse or romantic partners, a friend or family member.

Connect with your trading plan

Update your trading plan week by week or month to month to incorporate new thoughts and kill awful ones. Return and read the arrangement at whatever point you fall in an opening and are searching for an approach to get out.

Be careful with reinforcement

Dynamic trading discharges adrenaline and endorphins. These synthetics can create sentiments of happiness, notwithstanding when you are losing cash. Thus, this urges addictive characters to take terrible positions, just to get a hurry.

Try not to cut corners

Your opposition burns through many hours consummating methodologies and you are in for a severe shock in the event that you hope to toss a couple of darts and leave with a benefit. It's far more terrible in the event that you cut corners in a mind-blowing remainder since that unfortunate propensity is a lot harder to break.

Grasp simplicity

Concentrate on value activity, understanding that everything else is optional. Feel free to assemble complex; specialized markers yet remember their essential capacity is to affirm or disprove what you're prepared eye as of now observes.

Evade the obvious

Benefit infrequently pursues the greater part. When you see an ideal exchange arrangement, almost certainly, every other person sees it too, planting you in the group and setting you up for disappointment.

Arrange your personal life

Whatever is not right in your life will, in the end, persist into your trading execution. This is particularly risky on the off chance that you haven't profited, riches and the attractive extremity of plenitude and shortage.

Try not to break your rules

You make trading principles to get you out of inconvenience when positions go seriously. On the off chance that you don't enable them to carry out their responsibility, you have lost your order and opened the entryway to significantly more noteworthy misfortunes.

Tune in to your intuition

Trading utilizes the scientific and imaginative sides of your cerebrum, so you have to develop both to prevail over the long haul. When you are alright with math, you can upgrade results with reflection, a couple of yoga stances or a tranquil stroll in the recreation center.

Make peace with losses

Trading is one of only a handful couple of callings where losing cash each day is a characteristic way to progress. Each trading misfortune accompanies a significant market exercise in case you are available to the message.

Try not to believe in a company

In case you are excessively enamored with your trading vehicle, you offer an approach to defective basic leadership. You must gain by wastefulness, profiting while every other person is inclining the incorrect way.

Lose the crowd

Long haul productivity requires situating in front of or behind the group, yet never in the group since that is the place savage techniques target. Avoid stock sheets and visit rooms. This is not kidding business and everybody in those spots has an ulterior thought process.

Try not to get even

Drawdowns are a characteristic piece of the merchant's life cycle. Acknowledge them effortlessly and adhere to the reliable methodologies you realize will in the long run, recover your presentation on track.

Try not to count your chickens

Like an exchange that is going your direction, yet the cash is not yours until you closeout. Lock in what you can as ahead of schedule as possible, with trailing stops or fractional benefits, so concealed hands cannot pickpocket your prosperity ultimately.

Watch for early warnings

Huge misfortunes once in a while happen without various specialized admonitions. Dealers routinely overlook those signs and enable would like to supplant keen control, setting themselves up for torment.

Apparatuses don't think

Dealers compensate for deficient aptitudes with costly programming, prepackaged with a wide range of exclusive purchase and sell signals. These apparatuses meddle with important experience since you think the product is more brilliant than you are.

Play with your head

It's normal for dealers to copy their monetary saints, but at the same time, it's an ideal method to lose cash. Take in what you can from others; at that point, back off and set up your very own market personality, in light of your one of a kind abilities and risk resistance.

Things That Affect the Price of Options

There are a few factors that affect how options are priced. These are implied volatility, the price of the underlying asset, time until expiration, and it's in or out-of-the-money status.

Implied volatility is the forecast of how the price of a security will perform in the future. If the security is more volatile, it means that the price will move dramatically. Volatility is about market fluctuations. In bearish markets, the implied volatility increases because it is believed the price will fall; in a bullish market, the implied volatility decreases. The number can only tell you how much it is believed that the price will change, but it will not tell you in what direction.

The price of the underlying asset affects how premiums are set because they have to be in some vicinity of the asset's price. So an option for a stock which is expensive will be expensive, while for one that is cheap will be cheap. However, this has no bearing on whether or not the option will be profitable, and it makes sense for the option to be priced at a price that is close to the value of the underlying asset since, in the end, you will decide whether to buy or sell the underlying asset.

The time before expiration is also important in determining the price of the premium paid for an option. The more time until expiration, the more expensive the option will be. This is because there is more time for the price of the underlying asset to move into territory that may be profitable for the person who owns the option. The issuer of the option holds more risk, so they charge more for the option. The less time there is, the less the option will cost because there is less time for the underlying asset price to move in a vicinity that may be profitable to the person who holds the option.

The moneyness of the option pertains to whether or not the underlying option is in-the-money or out-of-the-money. An in-the-money option will be more expensive than one that isn't. This is because there is a perceived starting position that is favorable to the option holder. At the same time, it looks like the issuer is in a losing position already from the beginning. As we have seen, options work because the writer of the option and the holder are betting against each other.

Tips for Success

Most successful traders have tips and tricks that they employ to ensure they make some good profit trading options. Here are some of them.

Understand technical and fundamental analysis

Before you start trading, ensure that you carry out an analysis of the market. Technical analysis involves the study of how the price is expected to change. The idea behind this concept is that you can study historical patterns in price changes and determine how the price may change in the future.

Always be flexible when trading options

When you are working with stocks and some of the other securities out there, you will need to do it on the idea of buying low and selling high. But when you are working with options, this approach often doesn't meet all of your needs. With options, you can profit even if the market is going down.

Working with break-even points

Another thing to consider when it comes to options trading is the break-even points. As a trader, you must understand these break-even points, so you know the best time to get out of a trade, and you don't exit too early and take a loss without even realizing it. The break-even point is often going to be specific, whether it's high or low, that the stock needs to reach before you can start to earn a profit.

Always do your research

Before you enter into any trade with options, make sure that you do sufficient amounts of research. Charts are going to be crucial when you work on your technical analysis. But this isn't always enough on its own. When you begin, take some time to figure out what kinds of stocks and underlying assets interest you the most, and then do some further research into those particular assets. Take your time to learn about the markets that you want to enter. Watch the charts and find out how they work.

Start with enough capital

You should always leave a little bit of money in your trading account. This is going to help you out when you are in the middle of a trade and can make it easier for your broker to keep working on trades without having to worry about a delay while your fund's transfer. The most successful traders in options will always check their accounts and make sure that they keep enough capital there so that even if there are a few bad trades along the way, they still have that nice cushion to rely on to help them.

Avoid the really big risks

It is true in investing that the higher the risk, the higher the reward. This may be the way to invest for some people, but for the average trader, it is going to spell disaster. If you want to be able to say that you are profitable with options trading, then you need to make sure that you keep your risks to a minimum as much as possible.

Trade at the right times

Since you are going to learn how to avoid big risks when you are an options trader, you are going to learn how to be very careful about your timing when it comes to entering and exiting the market. You have to be able to read the market the right way so that you are able to learn the best time to do both of those tasks. These investors have spent their time doing some research and they know how to look at the big picture, rather than always calling up the broker and hoping that they can trust that person.

Come up with your own plan

You also need to make sure that you are picking out a plan that is unique to you and that has things that you are willing to follow. While there is nothing wrong with listening to some experts in the field and considering what they say, it is never a good idea to just follow exactly what they say without considering it or thinking it through. What works for someone else may not completely work for you, so think things through before you just jump right in.

Learn how to be focused

Some of the most successful traders on the market are the ones who are able to keep themselves focused on the task at hand. There are quite a few people who have an idea that options trading is super easy, and then they jump in and become overwhelmed by what they are dealing with. If you are not used to this kind of investment, it may seem a bit hard to deal with in the beginning.

Never follow the crowd

Following the crowd is one of the quickest ways to lose money on the market. If you are looking at some of the trends that come up with the market, you will notice that the crowd hits on when things are too late. Options trading can get you on at the ground floor, offering you a good discount on the item or asset that you want and can yield a good profit if you play your cards right. This is something that you are only able to do if you think for yourself and do not fall into the trap of following the crowd.

Your exit point, or your escape plan

As part of your trading plan, you must have a clearly defined exit strategy, one that you stick with no matter what. To keep this simple, that exit point is the place where you will close out the trade and walk away if the business starts to head south and you start to lose money. If you follow this, you can protect your investment, and it ensures that you don't stay in the market for too long.

Have enough capital

The reason why most beginners do not make it in options trading is not having enough capital. Most people get excited at how easy options trading can be and think that they can make an instant profit from their little capital in a matter of days. However, before they realize it, a few trades have swallowed their capital. They are then left with nothing to trade on. To be on the safe side, start with a good amount of cash that can sustain you for a number of trades.

Get a suitable trading style

What differentiate traders is their preferences, personalities, and trading styles. You need to understand the style that suits you best. For example, some traders prefer working at night, while others are more effective in day trading. Some of the traders will make several short sales during the day, while others will factor in the issue of time and volatility just to gain a large profit over periods that may last between few days and a month.

Create a risk management plan

Having a plan is vital for your success. You need to have it in place before you start trading. Remember, options are high-risk tools, and it is important to have strategies in place that can help you minimize the risks involved with each trade. Use your money wisely.

Diversify the stocks you trade in to reduce the potential of losing all your capital. Most of the expert traders only seal a contract when there are low risk and high profits.

Be patient and disciplined

To succeed in options trading, you must develop a high sense of discipline. Carry out extensive research and set the right goals. Stick to these goals and have them in mind as you seize trading opportunities. Be careful that you do not follow the crowd and don't believe in some facts and opinions before doing some research.

Patience and discipline will help you stick to your capital and risk management plans. These attributes also assist you to avoid trades you are not successful in.

Understand the market cycle

The options trading market keeps changing every time. You need to remain updated on the market trends and make the necessary adjustments to your plan accordingly. Through constant learning, you will be able to learn new strategies and identify better trading opportunities that other traders bypass.

Understand when to trade and when to exit. Know when the market is taking an uptrend or declining. Follow and interpret Forex news to understand what to expect in the future and where the industry is heading.

Keep records

Having a record of your past trades can help you determine when to make a call or put an option successfully. Some of the successful traders keep records of all their transactions. Analyzing these records continuously can help you identify vital patterns in the options you are trading in. It can also help improve your odds in the trade.

Identifying a Reliable Broker

There are plenty of brokerage firms available online. These brokerage firms provide traders like you with a platform to trade safely. These firms charge you a fee to access the platform and carry out your trades. They also provide you with tools that you need to trade successfully and customer service.

Generally, the lower the fees or commission charged, the less the customer service and assistance you can expect. On average, you should expect to pay between $2 and $5 per options contract that you invest in.

Sometimes you will be asked if you prefer a cash or margin account when opening an account with a broker. A cash account means you will trade using your own money. On the other hand, a margin account allows you access to credit facilities where you borrow money from the broker to invest in certain securities. Keep in mind that you are only able to borrow money from your broker against certain securities like bonds, stocks, and mutual funds.

You will not be able to borrow to invest in stock options because they are strictly cash-only trades. Options also settle trades the very same day or one business day. Therefore, you will require substantial cash amounts to enter trades. When you enter complex trades, you will also need to set some cash aside just in case you are obliged to buy shares at a certain price.

When opening an account, ensure that you choose a broker that rates you:

At this level, you are able to trade in options, even as a beginner. Also, tick on the margin box rather than cash just so that you always have access to borrowing from the broker. There are generally four levels of traders. They range from level 0 to level 3.

At level 3, you are allowed to enter profitable but risky trades. For instance, you can participate in naked calls and naked puts. You can also participate in other more complex trades. However, risky trades will require much higher deposits, so keep this in mind. All in all, brokers are all different. However, they will all need you to have access to cash and stocks in your account. This way, you will be able to fulfill your obligations and trade as often as you need to. Therefore, you will access options markets via your broker. Your broker will usually have access to the major platforms where options are traded, such as the Chicago Board Options Exchange.

Types of Brokers

We have different kinds of brokers. There are two main types. These are discount brokers and full-service brokers. A full-service broker, also known as a traditional broker, provides a wide variety of services to clients. These services include personalized advice to clients about where to invest or place their money. These professionals serve mostly active traders who prefer to make their own financial decisions.

On the other hand, we have discount brokers who are more suited to traders who know what they are doing and wish to manage their affairs. As such, clients pay only a minimal amount and, in return, get to make most, if not all, their financial decisions. What they do mostly is to execute orders from clients like you. This means that when you enter a trade or a position, the broker will execute these on your behalf.

You are also likely to encounter brokerage firms that provide a combination of these services. They generally offer a bouquet of services from which clients get to choose the services they desire. A lot of options traders, including beginners and novices, prefer the discounted services. Any trader that is confident enough to trade on their own and implement options strategies is very likely to be successful.

Speed of trades execution and availability

A good platform should also be responsive. There is no need for spending so much time coming up with a strategy only for the platform to fail you. Ensure that you find a good platform that is sufficiently responsive, so that you do not lose any advantages based on your analysis. Also remember to ensure that you have an excellent system from your PC or laptop computer to system, applications, and connectivity. These are crucial for successful trading experience.

Ease of Use

Another crucial aspect of any trading platform or online brokerage is its ease of use. All too often, brokerage firms will present quite complex or oblique platforms that take a while to master. Some keys may be spread apart, while some functions are complex and hard to master. Such platforms are not ideal for traders.

Fees and Commissions

Also crucial are fees, including commissions, penalties, and so on. It is crucial to find an affordable broker whose costs and charges are minimal. If you are not careful, fees will eat into your profits. As it is, options brokerages are super careful to stand out from the competition.

CHAPTER 3:

QUICK AND ACCURATE BASICS OPTION TRADING STRATEGIES

Long Calls

Options terminologies can seem confusing, but once you understand the basics, you will be good to go. Long simply means to buy, and short means to sell. A long call option gives you the right to buy an underlying stock at strike price A. It offers you the opportunity to get your game right without getting wiped out directly if you were to be trading directly in the stock market.

If you are feeling bullish about a stock (meaning that you hope that a specific stock will rise in value at a point in the future), you can choose to buy the stock outright or use a long call option. You will profit in a long call option when the stock rises according to your prediction. But if the opposite happens, you will only lose your premium paid.

Apart from that, long calls are less expensive as compared with buying the stock outright. If you were to be investing in the stock market, a failure for a stock to rise could just get you absolutely disappointed. You will encounter a lot of risks since you have already bought part ownership into the company.

If you consider entering the market through a bullish strategy, you need to ensure you thoroughly analyze the time horizon a chosen stock moves in a specific direction and the number of points required for that stock price movement. To minimize risks, what most people do is to buy more short term out of the money calls. This can be dangerous if all those calls have not moved successfully to indicate a gain.

The first place to enter the market is through long calls options. Most beginner options traders enter the market through this area due to its simplicity. Sometimes it might very be challenging to make a profit through long calls, but then it is still not complicated like the advance option trading strategies.

Risk/reward analysis for long call options strategy

The following entails the risks and rewards to have in mind while using this strategy:

It involves a little money, making it attractive for beginner options traders. It helps stock traders to manage their portfolio and avoid trading in stocks that are expensive to buy.

The loss made is only limited, that is if the underlying stock falls, instead of rising. It helps to risk a little money than to lose, all in an underlying stock trade.

There is no need for any complex calculations before executing the stock options plan.

It does not involve margin debt and it also has lower commissions as compared with other complex option trading strategies.

Avoid using all your money in a long call option. Buying many out of the money call options because it is cheap can make you lose your trading capital.

You need to understand that the call option is subject to time decay, which depreciates with the passing time towards expiration.

Simple calculations for Long Call Options

To minimize your losses and maximize your gains, you need to do a simple calculation to have an overview of how the entire long call options work. A breakeven point is to realize if the underlying financial instrument has neither made a loss or a gain. The following example will help you understand this better.

Source: Schwab Center for Financial Research (Strategy at Expiration)

- Long 1 GYZ June 50 Call @ $ 4
- Maximum Loss =$ 400.00 (4.00 option premium paid x 100 shares per contract)
- Breakeven Point =$ 54 (4 option premium + 50 strike price)
- Maximum Gain = Unlimited

To calculate the profit potential before aspiration: Profit = [(Rise in underlying stock) x delta value] / price of call options

The problem with a long call option is that it has a limited life span. Therefore, the underlying stock must move upward very fast above the breakeven point in order to generate unlimited gains for the owner. The downside is that the owner of the options stands to lose premium when the underlying stock hasn't moved upward as expected.

Short Call Options Strategy

A short call options strategy is where an options trader is betting on the fact that a particular price of an asset is going to drop and therefore placing an option on it. In this case, an options trader is taking a bearish position (he or she is forecasting or predicting that a particular financial instrument) will drop in pricing rather than go down).

Instead of buying calls, an options trader will rather be selling calls, which gives the holder the right to buy the underlying security at a given price. This is how a short call option works. It operates by the mode that if underlying security falls, the short call option will generate a profit for the owner.

In the case where the underlying security falls, it will merely give unlimited exposure to the owner at the time value of the option, making the call naked. This happens when the short call trader does not particularly own the underlying security. To cut losses, experienced options trader ensures they own the underlying security while betting against the market, thus creating a covered call.

Simple calculations for short call options

- Long 100 GYZ June 50 Call @ $ 4
- Maximum Gain =$ 500.00 (5.00 option premium received x 100 shares per contract)
- Breakeven Point =$ 55 (5 option premium + 50 strike price)
- Maximum Loss = Unlimited

To calculate the loss potential before aspiration: Loss = [(Rise in underlying stock) x delta value] / price of call options

In this example, let's say that you own shares of GYZ Company. The stock is trading at $4 per share and you notice that the share price is likely to go down after your technical and fundamental analysis on the stock market. Since you are feeling bearish about the stock and betting that GYZ stock will go down, you decided to sell shares of the company to Daniel Electricals Inc.

You sold a call for $ 5 per share, which amounted to an amount of $500 premium, creating a portfolio income for that asset. You collected the upfront premium money. What happens next? After a few days, the shares become to take an upward movement on the stock market. The share per stock moved from $4 per share to $ 7 per share. In this case, your analysis has gone against you.

Daniel Electricals Inc. can decide to exercise a naked shorting call and buy the underlying stock at $ 5 per share, they will net $ 700, generating a profit of $ 200 on their trading activities. Whilst you will take a losing position. On the other way, if the stock price drops to $ 2 per share, you will make a profit of $ 2 per share, netting $200.00.

Long Puts/Buying Put Options Strategy

A long-put strategy works in the same way as a long call. But in this case, you are taking a bearish position on the stock price movement in the market. Instead of betting on the fact that a stock price will be going down, you notice an upward trend in the movement of stocks through fundamental or technical analysis of publicly traded stocks in the financial market.

Just as a short call option strategy, you have to be right about the stock price movement direction, the magnitude, and the time frame for that change for you to make a profit in the market. There are many reasons for a trader to buy a short put. One of such reasons is hedging against potential loses in stock value due to the high amount of volatility in the market.

If an underlying asset falls in value, you can choose to buy a put option, which increases in value to offset the underlying loss. A long put option works as a protective put or married put. This is the reason you should use a put option only when you are feeling bullish about a particular stock.

Example of Long Put Option

An investor has long (bought) shares of XYZ Company at $ 50 per share. After holding the shares for some time, the investor feels bullish about the stock after a fundamental and technical analysis of the market and then decided to buy a put to hedge against the potential losses in the shares.

The strike price of the underlying stock was at $ 40 for $ 2.00 premium, generating profits of $ 200.00 for 100 shares of stock. In this case, even if XYZ Company falls in stock price, the only thing they will lose is $ 1,200 shares. The shares of stock are said to be a hedge against losses in the marketplace.

The trading strategy used here is that the underlying stock will increase in value when the main stock price falls in value. However, if the stock option has been exercised by the buyer, it will put the seller short of the underlying stock. This will mean the trader will have to buy back more of the underlying to realize a profit from that stock.

Alternative repair strategy

In this strategy, rather than rolling down into a bull call spread, you would instead roll down into a butterfly spread. To continue with the previous example, this would be useful if Microsoft dropped to $90. If this occurs, you would then want to sell the July $90 calls at $4 a piece while retaining ownership of the original long call for July $95. This will also require that you purchase a July call at $85, which should sell for around $7.30 once you factor in time decay.

When it comes to the downside of this scenario, the total amount of risk actually drops as the sum total when it comes to the debit amount is only $230, and these are also less upside risks when the underlying asset begins to return towards the breakeven point. It is also important to keep in mind that if the stock stays the same, the options trade will still successfully generate a profit.

Combined Repair Strategy

This strategy is a variation of the common butterfly spread, which means, returning the earlier example once more, that in the previous example, the maximum amount of profit you could expect to see would be the result of the strike price of the two $90 July short calls that were generated. However, if the movement leads to prices dropping away from this point to the point that losses are generated instead, then you may also find success by combining the two previous repair strategies to create a multifaceted approach which can be used to help maintain the types of ideal odds that tend to come along with ensuring a profit from an almost certain loss.

Consider the Strike Price

If you want to use this strategy as effectively as possible, it is important to ensure you start with an accurate strike price when it comes to the options you are considering. This is extremely important as the price will always determine the true cost of the trade while also playing a large factor in your ultimate breakeven point. The best way to start in most cases will be by first looking at the magnitude of the potential unrealized loss you are ultimately recovering from. As an example, if you purchased an underlying asset for $40, which is now only worth $30, then your loss would be equal to $10 per share.

In this instance, you would then need to purchase a call that is already at the money while also writing a call that is out of the money aimed at a higher overall strike price that is higher above the initial strike price of the calls that were originally purchased. Keep in mind that you need to purchase the related calls at a strike price that is half of the anticipated loss in order to come out on top. As such, you would want to plan on working with three-month options for the best results. As a general rule, the greater the loss you are recovering from, the longer it will take you to repair the damage.

Likewise, you will also need to understand that you won't get out of all mistakes scot-free as some mistakes will require a debit of one type or another in order for the setup to work properly. Furthermore, if you end up experiencing losses of greater than 70 percent, then you will have to be very lucky, or very good, to recover completely.

Time to Unwind

While breaking even will be enough in some situations, other times, you will still be able to turn things around to the point that you can still turn a profit. As an example, assume that you purchased an underlying stock for $60, which dropped to $50 for a time before robustly bouncing back to $65, which means you now no longer want to sell when it hits $70.

In order to unwind this position successfully, and turn a profit in the interim, you will want to close out a positive that has been previously working to offset additional investments. Unwinding will increase liquidity in some instances, and if an asset is less liquid, it can then be difficult to move, which increase the related liquidity risk as well. It doesn't matter if this transaction was set up deliberately or occurred by chance; all risks associated with the security will still apply when it comes to unwinding it successfully.

Unwinding proves even more beneficial when the volatility of the underlying stock is on the rise, and you still want to hold the stock as well. You should then find that your options are in a much more attractive position as long as you work to maintain a positive position with the underlying stock as well.

Keep in mind that it is possible for issues to arise in this scenario, if you try and exit the strategy while the stock is still greater than or equal to the breakeven price, as this will surely cost you because the value of the option will continue to be negative in this instance. Thus, the best course of action is going to be unwinding cautiously when a given position has a price that is lower than the first breakeven price. This is only the case, however, if all of the related prospects are promising at the time. If this is not the case, then the best course of action will typically be cutting your losses and starting a new position with the same stock at the new market price.

Covered Call Strategy

In this strategy, a trader buys a stock, and then they write a call option for that stock. The strategy generally works well on a stock that the investor is going long on. This means this is not a stock that you wish to speculate, but you would still like to receive some income on it while you keep it. And if you do sell it, you will sell it at a higher cost.

Here is the strategy in action. Say you own 300 shares of Lemonade Inc. that are currently going at $1.50. Then you write a call option at the strike rate of $1.70 per share. The premium you charge for this is 15¢ per share. If the stock price rises past $1.70 before expiration, let's say it is $1.90, the person to who you sold the call option to, will exercise their call option. You will be forced to sell 300 shares at the price of $1.70 per share, but since they will be paying a premium of 15¢ per share, you are selling your shares at $1.85 per share (strike price + premium), which is still high. The 5¢ that is left over is not the money that you lose. It is just money you missed out on. If the price of Lemonade Inc. stock does not rise sufficiently for the call option to be exercised, you will collect on the premium and still keep your shares. Regardless of what happens, you will leave with more money than you started with.

It is a very good strategy to use if you intend to keep the stock for a long time, and you don't think the price will increase that much in the near future but still want to collect some money on that stock.

This strategy is also referred to as a buy-write strategy. This even sounds better.

Bull Call Strategy

A bull call strategy is when a trader uses two call options on the same underlying asset, one with a lower strike price and the other with a higher strike price. The trader buys a call option above the current market price. Then they simultaneously sell a call option that has a higher strike price. These two call options share the same expiry date. What this does is that it reduces the price of the call option you have bought. Since you believe the underlying stock will not rise significantly, you collect on a premium that gets deducted from the amount you have spent on a call option. This allows you to benefit from small price increases, but it also has the effect of capping the maximum price you can make on a trade. Let's look at our Lemonade Inc. example.

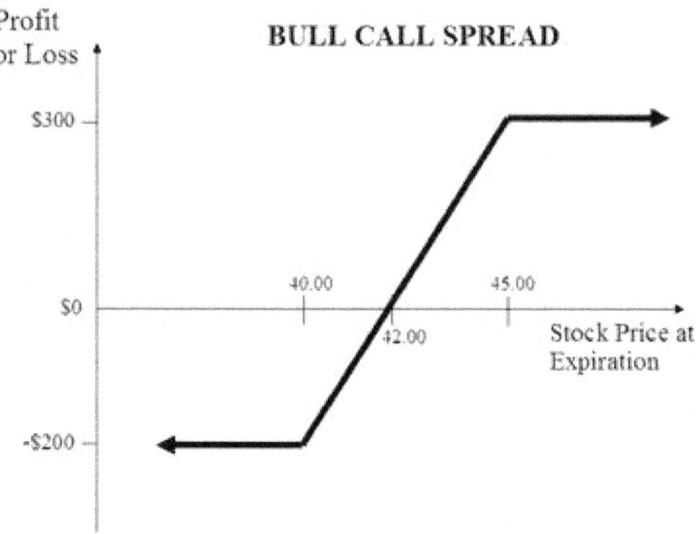

Mark looks at Lemonade Inc. stock currently trading at $1 per share, and he believes that the price of the stock will increase. There is a call option with a strike price of $1.20 per share that is currently selling at 50¢ per share. This means that for Mark to realize a profit, the stock price of Lemonade Inc. would have to rise above $1.70. This means the call option is very expensive. To limit the cost of the call option and also gain profit from the price movements, Mark buys the call option but simultaneously sells a call option for the same stock at 20¢ per share at a strike rate of $1.90. Now he can subtract the 20¢ he gets in premiums from the 50¢ he spent on the first call option. Meaning he has now spent 30¢ for the call option, the stock only has to rise above $1.50 for Mark to begin collecting a profit. This has another effect if the stock price rises above $1.90, Mark would have to sell his stock if the call option bought from him is exercised, which means that mark can only make a profit in the range between $1.50 between $1.90. This is where his profit is capped.

If the price of the stock does not rally, Mark has only spent 30¢ a contract for a call option that could have cost him 50¢ each ($30 instead of $50 in premiums), he does not lose that much. But if the stock rose, the maximum amount Mark could make per share is 40¢ (so $40 per call option since one call option bundles a hundred shares). The bull spread strategy is mainly bullish, as the name suggests. Investors using this strategy are confident that the price will go up and make trades that take advantage of upward movement at the lowest cost to them.

Bear Put Spread

To get started with this kind of strategy, you will want to pick out the right stock that will fit into the criteria that is needed for this strategy. Remember that for this strategy, you want to have a negative outlook on the chosen stock. You want a stock that is going to go down for some reason, whether you have heard some bad news about the stock or there is something else that is going to bring the value of your stock down.

After you have been able to pick out the right stock, you will need to purchase one slightly OTM put option. You will also want to sell one OTM put option, making sure that the strike price ends up being about one or two strikes lower than the option that you purchased in the first step. You also want to make sure that you are picking out ones that have the same stock and the same expiry date as what you did with the first step.

Once you are done with all of these trades, you want to make sure that you monitor your position and watch what is going on. You will then want to get out of both positions once they have helped you to receive significant profit, which is about 30 to 40 percent of the maximum potential profit.

This one is going to work similar to what you were able to do with the bull call spread. If you decide to increase the spread, you are going to increase how much potential profit you are able to make, but it also increases the risks that you are dealing with. In addition, you can choose to decrease the spread, the risk will also decrease, but you would also limit how much profit you could potentially make on the trade.

There are a few times when you will choose to trade using the bear put spread. You will want to go with this kind of strategy when the market has a pretty negative outlook on the stock that you want to use. This is usually going to happen when some development occurs, such as the company not making the earnings that it should, or the organization has made some new changes or decisions that the investors did not look at favorably.

Some people choose to trade with this kind of strategy when the company is part of or is selling under pressure. They do not want to sell, but there is something that is going on that will make them feel like they do need to sell. For example, there may be some environment or market conditions that are unfavorable to the company that surfaced and is changing the company.

Remember that since the bear put spread is considered a debit spread strategy, you will have to work with the time-decay, and it is going to go against your overall position, even though this kind of decay is considered a lot slower than what will happen with a naked long put position.

When it comes to the disadvantages and advantages, this spread is going to end up being pretty similar to the bull call spread. The primary advantage that comes with this trade is that the ratio for risk and reward is pretty good and even a moderate decrease on a stock can still help you to earn some good profits.

You will also be able to increase the amount of profit that you could potentially make by widening up the spread. To do this, you will want to increase the strike price that happens between your two options. You can also choose to reduce your risk in order to help you out as a beginner, and to do this, you will decrease the spread. In order to decrease the risk, you will want to decrease the number of strike prices that are going on between the two options.

The biggest disadvantage that comes with this strategy is dealing with the time decay that will work against the position. And while there is a limited amount of potential loss, if the stock ends up staying stagnant for a long period of time, the position is going to end up with a loss.

Let's take a look at how the bear put spread strategy is going to work. In this case study, the trade is entered on the 18th of May, and we are going to use Nifty 50 again, and we will have about seven days to expiry left for this kind of option.

There are a number of reasons why you would want to use this for the bear put spread strategy.

During the last month, the Nifty index has shown a good amount of rise, a rise that has been going in line with some of the positive global cues in the market. However, there is still a strong resistance at the 9500 mark, and while the market has let this stock stay around this mark for a bit of time now, it isn't showing any signs of being able to go above that mark. It is also trading on a narrow range, so this makes it perfect for this option.

Since there are less than seven days to go before the expiry of the May month options contract, it looks like some profit booking would take place, and there might be some corrections that happen in the near term. In addition, this stock has some premium options that are cheaper since there are only a few days to expiry, and a bull put spread can be entered into with a low amount of risk while still being pretty successful for you.

So, let's take a look at some of the steps that you need to take in order to finish this trade.

The first thing that you need to do is to pick out the right option and stock that you want to trade with. For this strategy, there are a few conditions that need to be met to make sure you will see success, including:

The overall risk of your position should never be more than three percent of the total amount of capital that you have to use. Since there are only seven days until expiry on this option, the prices for these options are going to be provided to you at a discount, so there is not really a reason to risk as much as you would with some of the other strategies that we have chosen.

Since we are only expecting a moderate correction of less than 100 points with this stock, the slightly OTM higher strike put option should not be more than 30 to 40 points below the market price of the chosen stock. At the time of the trade, the market price was 9460.

If you take the above criteria into consideration, the trader would decide to trade the 9450 put option, and the 9300 put option, with purchases of 40.75 and 13, respectively.

The total risk to this one is going to be around 2081, which ends up being about 1.2 percent of the capital that is available for this trader. This is lower than the three percent that is recommended, so you are staying within the limits that you are given.

The second step that you should take is to purchase the OTM put option. For this one, the 9450 PE, with the May expiry, was bought at 40.75. You will also want to sell an OTM put option that has a lower strike price.

The 9300 PE for Nifty, which is three strikes lower than that 9450 that we had talked about before. Here is a summary of the trade position that the trader used for this strategy below:

Summary Table		
Stock or Index Traded	Nifty	
Lot size for each option	75	
Option 1 Higher-strike Put Option - Buy	Strike Price	9450
	Premium Paid	40.75
Option 2 Lower-strike Put Option - Sell	Strike Price	9300
	Premium Received	13.00
Difference Between any 2 Consecutive Strikes-prices		50.00
Max Profit		9,169
Max Loss		2,081
Condition for maximum profit	Stock price at time of expiry < Strike Price of lower-Strike put option	
Condition for maximum loss	Stock Price at time of expiry > Strike Price of higher-strike put option	
Break-even	Stock Price at expiry =	₹ 9,422.25

Going off the information that is listed above, the maximum profit that you will be able to earn if this stock falls below 9300 at your time of expiry would be 9168.75. And then the maximum amount that the trader would lose if the stock goes or stays above the 9450 at the time of expiry would be 2081.25. The break-even point price that you need to reach in order to earn at least some sort of profit would be 9422.25.

Let's take a look at the profit and loss payoff diagram below in order to find the profit and loss of this kind of trade plotted against five different expiry prices for that particular stock.

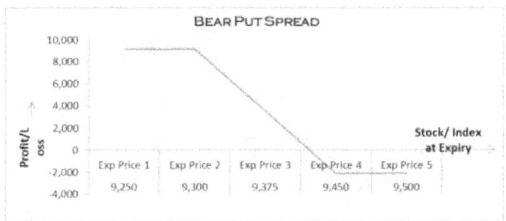

Let's see the results of the trade. After just being in the market or a day, this stock ends up going down by over sixty points, which means that the price of both of these put options went up. Since the trader did not think that the stock would go through and correct itself much further and that it may reverse its movement before too long, the position was closed by squaring of both legs on this trade and the profit was booked.

The trader could have gone through and stayed in the trade, but it was becoming more likely that the position would go back up, and then the trader would end up losing money from their position, so it was much better to leave the trade early on.

The return on investment was decent on this one. The ratio of the net loss or the net profit to the total sum that is invested in the trade will help you to learn the return on investment, or the profit percentage in this trade. Since the trader was able to put 40,000 into this trade and they were able to make a net profit that was 2,265.

By dividing the profit by the total amount of investment that the trader did for the trade, the profit ratio is going to be about five percent. This is a decent amount of return on investment, considering you stayed in the market for only a day or two at most. You may have been able to make more profit in the long run, but it is possible that the position could have turned as well, making it so that the trader would lose all of their money in the process. It is much better to get out quickly, especially since the expiry date is near in the future to start with.

Calendar Put Spread

The calendar spread on puts works the same way as it does with the call calendar spread. Generally, the call spread is utilized more than the put, unless there is a greater than expected decline in the market or the put spread gives a greater return than the call spread.

This is a market-neutral strategy and is excellent for sideways markets. Like with the call spread, the aim of this strategy is to sell the shorter term put and earn the premium while going long on the longer-term put.

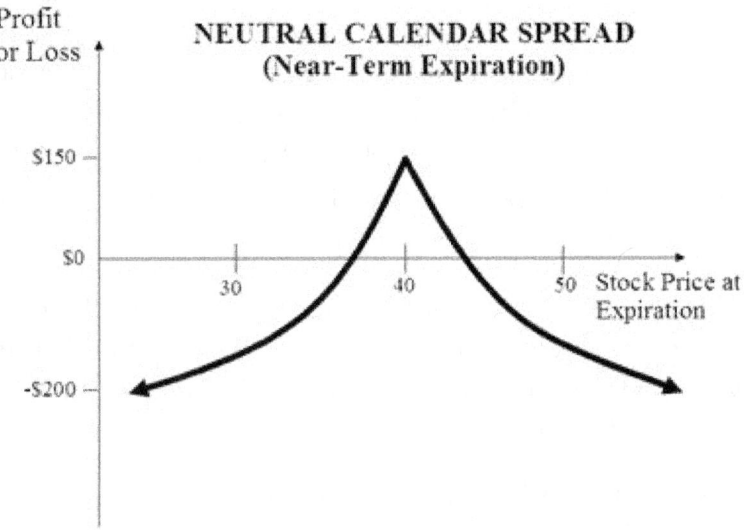

The trade has two legs to it: the short term put and the long term put. The first step is to identify a suitable short term put to write. Generally, if the price is near a support level and you're expecting it to meander a bit before declining in the longer term, you can choose an at the money or slightly out of the money option.

The exact strike price you choose depends on the distance between the current price and the support level ahead. If there is a gap, choose a strike price that is beyond the support level. Sticking with our example of AAPL, let's assume it is at a support level that is going to hold for the short term before folding in the medium term.

Currently, AAPL is trading at $181.30 so let's assume $180 is our support level for the short term. The current month $180 put is the most suitable to write, and doing this will fetch us a premium of $3.40.

The near month $180 put will cost $5.95 to go long on, and thus, our entry cost of the trade works out to:

Cost of trade entry/ Maximum loss per share= Premium paid for near month put-Premium received for current month put= 5.95-3.4= $2.55 per share.

The maximum reward, just like the call calendar spread, is something that depends on whether or not the stock falls below the support level over the medium term. If it does, you could exercise your near month option and ride the stock as it declines. Alternatively, you could trade the option itself and save yourself the commissions that arise from exercising it.

The factors to take into account for this strategy are much the same as the call calendar spread, except this is a bearish version of that strategy. You want to identify a level that the price is likely to remain above for the short term, but will dip below during the medium term.

The reward risk profile of this trade is excellent, and under the right market conditions, the calendar spread is a great strategy to deploy.

It might seem on the surface that a lot of the strategies replicate one another, but their individual risk profiles are different. So, make sure you work out the numbers prior to entering them or deciding which one is better. Generally speaking, you can follow the below guidelines to help you decide.

When calls become expensive, as in the case of a bull market on its last legs, bull call spreads work best. This is to capture whatever moderate level of gains there might be left. Of course, this presumes that you can read the decreasing strength of a trend well enough to deploy it in the first place.

In the final stages of a bear market, when volatility spikes and there aren't too many downside gains to be had, a bear call spread works the best. Bear markets tend to be shorter than bullish ones since the general public doesn't indulge in the short side. Thus, bear markets don't suffer from the over-enthusiasm that tends to push bull markets for longer than expected.

The bull put spread works like a charm in a sideways market when you are certain that the overall trend is still bullish, but currently, the stock is moving sideways or suffering from a bout of counter-trend enthusiasm. This is a good way to earn some income in the meantime and is a far safer option than trying to time a directional entry.

When a bear trend is accelerating to the downside, a bear put spread works the best. You could use this to hedge your positions in a long market, but that's not a trading strategy per se. As it is, using it in the manner described previously is your best bet of making some money off it.

The term comes from the way in which option chains are displayed. The strike prices are listed vertically with the puts and calls arranged on either side of them. Thus, the lower strike price is above the current price and the higher ones below.

So, by employing two legs on the trade, you're creating a vertical spread, as per the option chain table. With a calendar spread, you're on the same strike price, but visualizing a calendar, you're moving sideways or horizontally to the next month. Hence, the term horizontal spread.

You also would have noticed how some strategies, upon entry, pay you and some require an upfront cost. The ones that pay you are called net credit strategies and the ones that have a cost are called net debit ones. Net credit strategies pay you your maximum reward upfront, while net debit ones require you to wait for the maximum reward.

Of course, the flip side is that net debit strategies have you experiencing your full loss upfront, as opposed to net credit ones, where you need to see how it plays out. Take care to not develop a mental bias towards either one. All that matters is the market condition, not which one pays you first or last.

Naked Call Shorting

When it comes to call options, there are two main practices investors engage in naked shorting and covered shorting. Naked shorting has been ban by the SEC after the 2008 and 2009 market crash; however, there are loopholes that allow people to still engage in naked shorting activities, one of such is options trading.

So what is naked shorting? It is simply the practice of short selling shares that have not been affirmed that they exist. This is to say that the trader borrows the stock or make arrangements to borrow the stock. Based on those agreements made to acquire the stock, the person exercises short selling activities, even though the stock has not been own yet.

Sometimes some shares become less than the required demand in the market. In order to meet supply needs, some people adopt naked short selling, which has been considered illegal in recent times.

Trading activities tend to fail at the supposed time when the invested short selling underlying shares have not yet own or possess the said number of shares for the transaction to be completed. This is the reason it is important to analyze your risks when you are using a naked short selling strategy in an options trading.

There are potentially high risks involve in naked call shorting. Therefore it is very important to consider several factors before engaging in this method of trading. To be on the safer side, some investors adopt a covered call shorting rather than a naked call.

The Bear Call Spread

Next on the list is the bear call spread. This is another directional strategy that will be used by a trader when they believe that their underlying stock has reached its upper resistance level, and they do not believe that the underlying stock is going to go up much more at this point. They usually believe that the price point of the stock is going to stay flat and not change or it is going to go back down. Basically, this is going to be the opposite strategy that we talked about earlier with the bull put spread.

Like the bull put spread, the bear call spread is also a credit spread. What this means is the premium that you end up receiving while selling one leg of this trade is going to be greater than any premium that you end up paying for the second leg of the trade. You will end up receiving a net credit to your account when you decide to go with this position.

The first step that you need to take to create your bear call spread is to select the right stock that fits this kind of strategy. You will find that there are a variety of stocks that you can choose from, but you will need to pick based on your outlook for this kind of index.

Next, you will need to sell an OTM call option of the stock that you selected. And third, you should purchase an OTM call option that has the same expiry date and the same underlying stock as your id with your ATM call option, but the second one needs to have a higher strike price.

Once you enter the market, you will want to constantly monitor your position each day. Once you have made a considerable profit, which is about fifty percent of your max profit, it is time to exit your position. Or, once you have started to recognize some of the signs of the market and you are sure that the stock is not going to end up reversing, you could wait until the stock reaches its expiry and then take the maximum amount of profit.

There are some time periods that are better for entering a bear call spread than others. You would want to choose the bear call spread any time that you believe that your chosen stock is not likely to rise in price in the near future and that this stock is probably going to decline from its current price rather than go up. This can happen when the stock from a particular company that had big market expectations posted their results, and these were way below the expectations of the market. In addition, the index option could hit a big resistance level and this could cause it to go down a bit.

This method is not going to work that well if the stock is really volatile and it has the potential to rise quite a bit over the short term. You want to pick out some options that are not likely to go up anymore. You would then be able to use the bear call spread and make some profit whether the stock stays stagnant or the price goes down.

The maximum profit that you will be able to make with the bear call spread is when at the time of expiry, the stock price is trading below the strike price of the call option that was sold. To get the maximum profit, you will need to take the premium received or selling the lower-strike call option and minus the premium paid for purchasing the higher-strike call option. Then you can multiply both of these by the lot size.

The biggest loss that you would incur with this kind of spread is when at the time of expiry, the stock price is trading above the strike price call option you bought with the higher-strike price. This is why you want to make sure that you are picking out stocks that are going to go down or remain steady. If the stock goes up with this option, you will end up losing money in the process. This is why this strategy is a good one to choose if you think that the market is about to go down or you want to work with a stock that is not really increasing at the time.

The biggest advantage of working with the bear call spread is that it is going to ensure that the time-decay is going to work in your favor. As long as you go with a stock that is able to stay below your lower strike-price when the expiry happens, you will get the benefit of keeping your entire credit that you received when you entered into this position, and you have the potential to make a good profit.

However, there is a disadvantage of working with this strategy. With this position, if you see that there is the possibility that the stock will make a big movement that goes against your expectations. This means that the stock starts rising in price quickly rather than remaining stagnant or going down like you had predicted. If this does happen, the maximum amount that you could lose can be a lot more than the maximum profit that you might have been able to gain with this strategy, so there is some risk.

Here we are going to look at a case study of a trade that was done in May of 2017 for this strategy. The stock that was used for this option trade is the Nifty 50, and the type of exchange that was used was the NSE in India. The Nifty 50 is a good option to go with because it is considered a benchmark index on the Indian NSA. It is a diversified 50 stock index and will account for 12 sectors of the economy in India. It has some good stability, and the volatility that occurs with it daily is not that high.

The market at this time had gone through a long bull run, and it was about to run out of steam. The Nifty stock was showing signs of meeting some resistance when it reached the 9500 mark and it wasn't likely to cross over that barrier any time soon. This made it the perfect stock to work with the bear call spread, making sure that your resistance point was 9500.

The first step that you should take is to determine your options with the optimum strike-prices to trade. Since we found the resistance level to be bear the 9500 mark with this strategy, it was decided to sell an OTM option that was four strikes away from the spot price of Nifty. Since the spot price of this stock was at 9500 at the time of trading, the 9700 Nifty call options with a month expiry (so ending in June for this one) was picked to be written and to complete the second leg of the trade, the 9900 Nifty Call was selected.

With the help of a calculator in order to check the deltas, you would find that the delta of the lower-strike call is about 0.31. This implies that you are running the risk of 31 percent of the 9700 Nifty call reaching ITM at expiry time. This is a bit high for the risks than you should do, but since this index seems to have peaked, the risk was taken.

Now it is time to sell the OTM call option. The Nifty 9700 call option that was set to expire at the end of June was written for $46 to complete the first part of the trade. Then on the third step, the Nifty 9900 call option to expire at the end of June was bought for $9.80 to complete the second leg of the trade. Here is a chart to show what happened with this kind of trade:

Summary Table			
Stock or Index Traded		Nifty	
Lot size for each option		75	
Option 1 Lower-strike Call Option : Sell		Strike Price	9700.00
		Premium Received	46.00
Option 2 Higher-strike Call Option : Buy		Strike Price	9900.00
		Premium Paid	9.80
Difference Between any 2 Consecutive Strikes-prices			50.00
Max Profit			₹ 2,715
Max Loss			₹ -12,285
Condition for maximum profit		Stock/Index price at time of expiry <	9700
Condition for maximum loss		Stock/Index price at time of expiry >	9900
Break-even		Stock/Index at time of Expiry =	9,736.20

This table shows that the maximum profit you are able to make will be about $2,715 if the Nifty stock stays at or below the 9700 when the expiration occurs. However, the maximum loss that you could happen if the stock goes above the 9900 is 12,285. The break-even point that you would use here is the 9736.2, and as long as your index ends up over this point at the end of the trade, you would end up making a profit.

Here s a profit and loss payoff diagram that will show the profit and loss that you could earn plotted against five different prices for the index at expiration.

Results of the trade

With this case study, the Nifty stock did not go the way that the trader had hoped. Instead of moving down to 9500, it broke this resistance level and went up to 9700. Then the trading slowed down and it traded between the 9600 and 9700 range. Within a week, the 9700 call that sold for 46 had touched 80 before the premium came down to 70.

This trade position was left in a net loss for the following two weeks because of this development. However, this stock was not able to sustain itself over the 9700 level, and within three weeks, the time-decay brought in some erosion to your options. Three weeks into this four-week trend, the Nifty stock came down by about 25 points on its opening, and it was traded at the 9620. Because of this, the trader was able to exit the trade and make a profit.

With this one, the trader was able to earn a profit of 1087.50 if they exited at the three-week mark rather than waiting. There was some possibility of earning more profit by keeping the options for a bit longer and until the end of the month. But since the stock did go up unexpectedly, it is possible for this to happen again, and it is smart for the trader to choose to exit the market early and take some profit rather than running the risk of the stock going back up again and them losing all of their profit.

The return on investment in this option ends up being about 2.7 percent over the three weeks. This is not very high, but considering that the stock went against the expectations of the trader, it was better than the loss that they could have encountered. This still ended up being a profitable trade for the trader, despite things going up and against the wishes of the trader. In this one, the brokerages were not that high, so they have not been included into the calculations that we did to make things a little bit easier. You will have to pay a few fees for entering into these trades, but they are not too high and if you make good decisions with this trade, you will be able to cover them easily.

Short Put/Selling Put Options Strategy

A trader who writes a put option is referred to as the seller. In this case, an options trader will be required to buy the underlying stock and make sure everything is ready when the buyer is ready to exercise the option. A short put option is often referred to us naked or uncovered put since the seller is under obligation to purchase shares of the underlying stock before the buyer decides to exercise the right to the option.

Losses can be faced when the short put expires worthless without the underlying asset arising above the strike price of the put option. A short put should be used if you think that an underlying security will be able to rise up in price more than the strike price determined in the options contract.

To profit in options trading through a short put strategy, you need to ensure that the technical analysis conducted leads to a rise in stock price. When the price of the stock goes down in value over a period of the option, the option buyer can choose to exercise the right and hence making you incur potential losses.

However, you will make money through the premiums paid at the signing of the put options contract. Apart from making money through premiums by opening a put option, you can also be able to sell a stock at the underlying price in the financial market.

For example, say that a stock is currently selling at $ 100 in the financial market. You wish to buy the stock at $ 75. If you consider selling a put option at a strike price of $ 75 and receive a premium of let's say $ 2.00. If the price of the underlying stock drops to $ 75 as forecasted, then you will get to keep the premium while at the same time buying the underlying stock at the strike price.

The Importance of Volatility

While there are numerous reasons a person might want to start trading options on the regular, guaranteed returns are not one of them. There are a wide variety of different variables that can come into play when it comes to determining the premium for a given option, which means profits are never a sure thing. As such, if you are interested in trading options regularly, then you are going to need to do everything in your power to ensure you are aware of the implied volatility of a given asset to ensure you don't accidentally bite off more than you can chew.

Implied volatility can be thought of as the amount of volatility that you believe an underlying asset has, which means it will naturally be higher if the market is feeling bearish and as long as potential investors have a good reason to assume the asset is going to decrease in value at a point in the future. Meanwhile, if the market is feeling bullish, then you can anticipate the overall volatility to decrease as the market reacts to assumptions that the price of the asset is on the rise. This is due to the fact that most people naturally assume that bullish markets harbor less risk overall than markets that are bearish. This is what makes implied volatility so useful; it makes it possible for traders to reliably estimate the way the underly asset price is likely to move based on the overall state of the market and other types of predictive data.

Implied volatility is a factor in all types of asset trading but proves especially important when it comes to options trading as the greater the current level of implied volatility, the higher the related premium is going to do be. This is due to the fact that when an option is valued, implied volatility is already factored into the equation. Despite this fact, implied volatility is still just an estimate based on probability, which means it is more of a suggestion than a real indicator.

Despite this fact, many traders become overeager once they learn of it and treat it like the full-blown indicator it very much isn't. Thus if you can see the implied volatility for a given asset clearly you should feel safe in assuming that there are plenty of traders out there who can see the same thing and are already acting accordingly. Furthermore, implied volatility directly correlates to the current dominant opinion in the market, which is another pricing factor you will want to consider before making any serious moves.

When looking to implied volatility for answers, it is also important to understand that it does not actually predict the direction in which the price will be moving; only that change is coming. As an example, if the volatility of the asset is quite high, this typically means a price swing is on the horizon. However, the resulting swing could then be quite small, very large, or somewhere in between. If volatility is low, then this simply means that the price is likely to not make any changes that weren't clearly telegraphed.

Another common mistake that those who aren't familiar with implied volatility make is assuming it is similar to historical volatility when in fact the two are quite different. Historical volatility measures the previous changes the market has experienced and thus can have definitive results. As such, you are better off comparing the two types of volatility in order to understand the types of changes that the underlying asset in question is going to experience.

Key factors in determining implied volatility

The first factor you are going to want to be aware of in this instance is supply and demand, which affects implied volatility just as much as it does the market as a whole. While many traders rely on extremely complicated metrics to determine what trades to make and when it is important to keep in mind that the market still runs on the basic principles of supply and demand that it always did. As such, if you cut through the complicated theories and look for moments where supply and demand are extremely unbalanced, then you will always be able to make a profit no matter what. You will still need to learn as much as possible about the various strategies that you choose to move forward with, it is just important to keep in mind that the basics still apply.

In this case, if the demand for a security is especially high, then you can count on the implied volatility to be higher than normal as well. This, in turn, leads to higher than average premiums that come along with the added risk while the opposite remains true as well.

The next vital factor to consider is the time value that remains for the option in question as the shorter the remaining time for the option is the less implied volatility it will have left as well. This is due to the fact that the market assumes that with little time left, there isn't enough time for anything more to change for the underlying asset in the time left.

It is also important to understand that every option is going to have a different level of sensitivity when it comes to noticing changes in its implied volatility. As an example, the greater the amount of time value a given option has remaining, the lower its implied volatility will almost always be. Likewise, strike prices will always respond differently to implied volatility changes as strike prices that are closer to being in the money will naturally be more sensitive to volatility changes to those that are either in the money or very far out of the money. If you are unsure of how sensitive a given option is likely to be in the near future, the best way to double-check is to consider it's Vega (discussed in detail in the next chapter). Even still, it is important to not take the results as gospel as things could still change based on anything unexpected that hits the market between when you do your research and when you actually make your move.

Making the most of implied volatility

One of the best ways to figure out the implied volatility of any options you are working with is to take a closer look at the implied volatility chart that should already be a part of the trading platform you are currently using. Due to the fact that every stock is going to have its own range of implied volatility, it is important to analyze what you are working with regularly. When it comes to properly keeping tabs on these fluctuations, you will want to take a closer look at the various peaks and valleys the chart shows you like the points in-between tend to muddy the waters as opposed to actually clarifying things. It is also important to understand that implied volatility is always going to move in cycles, which means that for every period of low implied volatility that you experience, you are guaranteed to see another period when implied volatility is high as long as you wait long enough for it to materialize. Thus, by keeping these ranges in mind and forecasting the implied volatility of the assets you frequent on the regular, you should have a firm template for choosing more reliable trades on the regular. When determining a suitable strategy, these concepts are critical in finding a high probability of success, helping you maximize returns and minimize risk. If you are looking to forecast implied volatility, there are a few different things you should keep in mind. First, you need a way to accurately determine what the implied volatility is at the moment. The first thing you can do is to check the news to ensure you are up to date on anything that would explain the increase. As most movement is going to take place directly after these types of announcements, it is important to understand that anyone of the above is often enough to collapse the current level of implied volatility and zero it out.

CHAPTER 4:

ADVANCED STRATEGIES

Married Put

A married put strategy is when a trader or investor is in a long position on a certain stock, and then they buy a put option that has a strike price that is equal to the current market price. They do this to protect against depreciation or downward movement in the price. This means that the investor can be confident that they will gain from the price increase of their stock, and they can also enjoy the benefits of owning the stock. The benefits of owning stock are things like voting and getting paid dividends when profits are made. The bad news is that it costs somewhat to pay the put premium of the stock. When an investor does this, they are saying that they don't want to sell their stock below a certain favorable price, so in the event that the stock falls, they want to be made whole. It is more like insurance; the cost to the investor is the premium, limiting how much they lose on any given trade. The married put options, unlike the bull call spread, have unlimited profit potential if the stock performs well.

Let's say you are long on 2o0 shares of Lemonade Inc. When you bought these shares, they were at $1.50 each. Now, after months, the price of the shares has appreciated to $2.00. This is great. You have been enjoying some benefits of owning a stock like dividends and voting rights in the company. But you are worried about an announcement that Lemonade Inc. is going to make that could negatively affect the price of your stock. However, you still think there is a chance that this new direction could work in the company's favor, and you could make more money. In a sense, you are married to this stock, you are in for the long haul, but you don't want to lose a lot of money either if things go south. To protect your profits, you buy two put options, which give you the right to sell 200 shares at $2.00 each. The put option costs you a premium of 30¢ per share. Meaning if you exercise the put option, you will collect a profit of 20¢ per share compared to where you got in at $1.50 per share. But you will only decide to sell your shares at this position if you think that the position the company finds itself in won't be resolved, meaning you think the stock price will not recover before the expiration date of your put option.

If the price of the stock continues to rise as a result of the company's new move and favorable market, you get to keep your stocks and receive all the profit and benefits, having only lost the $60 premium on insurance in case things went badly. Now, you see how this strategy limits your losses but open you up to unlimited benefits. Losses are capped while profits are virtually limitless. While insurance on stock can be costly, it is not as costly as a market fall that does not rebound.

The Straddle and the Strangle

Long Straddle

The straddle is a very profitable strategy when it is used in a market where high volatility is expected. So, you know that the price will move sharply, but you don't know which direction it will go. Regardless, you want to profit from that movement. To profit from an upswing, you buy a call option. To benefit from a fall, you buy a put option for the same asset for the same expiration date at the same strike price. You realize a profit when the money you make is more than the premium you have spent on both options. Now let's return to a Lemonade Inc. example to show this.

Let's say that Lemonade Inc. stock is trading at $100 per share. But you believe because of the pending company announcement, the price will move sharply in either direction. So you buy a call option for a $10 premium per share and a put option for a $10 premium a share, both at a strike price of $100. You have $10,000 dollars in your account. This will cost you a total of $2,000 in premiums. So you are left with $8,000. The announcement is made before the expiry date of both options. Lemonade Inc. has experienced losses in the last quarter. Its stock fell by 30%, meaning it is now trading at $70 a share. In this situation, you can buy 100 shares at $70, costing you $7,000 and exercise your put option, selling them for $10,000. You have just made $3,000 on that transaction. You now have $11,000 in your account.

If the announcement made by Lemonade Inc. reports increases in sales and the stock rises by a record 50%, you will be in a position to buy 100 shares at $100 and then sell them on the market for $150 each. Since you have $8,000 leftover, you can't afford to exercise your call option. But you use your margin account to borrow $2,000 and buy the shares at $10,000. You make $15,000 on the transaction. You pay your debt, plus interest, it costs you $2,300. You are left with $12,700. You have made a profit of $4,700.

As you can see, no matter the direction the stock moves, as long as it is beyond the premium you spent on the options, you made a profit. But if the market price moves only slightly, you will have lost $2,000, and you will be left with $8,000 in your account.

Long Strangle

The strangle is similar to the straddle strategy, but instead of buying options that share the same strike price, asset, and expiry date, they buy two options that only share an expiry date and asset. So the strike prices are different from each other. It is also a strategy often used in situations that are similar to that of a straddle. In both cases, the trader believes that the price of the underlying stock will move in some direction, but they do not know which. They might have a slight bias about where it might go, but they exercise the strangle to catch profits if they're mistaken. Just like the straddle, if the price does not move enough, the money will be lost on premiums—time for that lemonade example. The situation is much like before. Lemonade Inc. will make an announcement, but the rumors around the report are positive, but investors are somewhat skeptical. For now, the stock price is stable, but once the announcement is made, the price might move sharply. Thinking the news might be positive, you buy a call option with a strike price at the current stock price. The stock is going at $100 per share. The premium costs you $10 a share. You think it is unlikely that the price will fall, but if it falls, you want some money for yourself. You buy a put option at a $98 strike price for $8 a share. You have spent a total of $1,800 on the premiums. Already, this strategy is cheaper than the straddle. If the price of the stock falls by 20%, you will collect a profit of $1,800, meaning you break even. If it rises sharply by 50%, you will rake in a profit of $5,000 from the transaction, that minus the premium paid is $3,200. If your bias was correct, you stand to make a few extra bucks that you would miss if using a straddle strategy. If your bias was wrong and the price falls sharply, you would still make money, but you will miss out on some of the action, although this doesn't translate to money lost. In both strategies, the price movement has to be sharp enough to overcome the premium spent. For instance, in a situation where Lemonade Inc.'s announcement doesn't sway the markets way, and they remain relatively stable, you will have lost $1,800, which is $200 less than you would have in a straddle strategy.

Here we are going to take a look at a case study using the long strangle in order to make a profit in options. This one was entered on the 8th of November in 2016 and the trader used the Nifty 50 stock.

During this time, there was a big political change around the world, and it was estimated that this would make some sort of impact over the global markets, at least for the short-term. This was the US election and many people were unsure about who would win. A win by the Democrats could add in some positive sentiment to the market, and it was expected that having the Republican candidate win would do the opposite. Either way, at the time it was looking as if the markets around the world would make a big change, either going up or down sharply. Because of the conditions, it looked like the perfect time to work with the long straddle and strangle strategy. The first step that you want to do with this is to pick out a good option to trade in. For this case, the traded decided to use the Nifty index and use the long strangle strategy. At the time, the Nifty index was trading at 8530, which meant that the closest OTM call option was going to be 8550 and the closest OTM put option would be the 8500. These two were the ones selected for the trade and the trader decided to pick an expiry date of the **24th** of November because this was the earliest expiring monthly service. At the time, the volatility of this index was much higher than it usually was at 14.9, the trader decided that it was worth taking the risk because the volatility of the whole market was supposed to rise even further before the big changes occurred, which would make the options more expensive overall. So, the second step that you need to do is purchase your slightly OTM call option, which would be the Nifty 8550. This was bought for 130. Then you can purchase the slightly OTM put option. This was the Nifty 8500 and it was purchased or 90. Let's take a look at the table below to see a little summary of the options that the trader used in this trade.

Summary Table			
Stock or Index Traded		Nifty	
Lot size for each option		75	
Option 1 ATM Call Option - Buy		Strike Price	8550
		Premium Paid	130.00
Option 2 ATM Put Option - Buy		Strike Price	8500
		Premium Paid	90.00
Difference Between 2 Consecutive Strikes			50
Max Profit			No Limit
Max Loss			16,500
Condition for maximum profit		No Upper Limit for Profits	
Condition for maximum loss		For Straddle: Stock Price at expiry = Strike Price of Options	
		For Strangle: Stock Price at expiry lies between Strike Prices of Option 1 & Option 2	
Break-even Points	Upper	Stock price at Expiry =	8,770.00
	Lower	Stock price at Expiry =	8,280.00

For this trade, the trader is able to make a maximum profit that is unlimited, but they do have a maximum loss. Here, the trader would potential would be 16,500 if they end up being wrong. This amount is going to be the premium amount that they paid in order to purchase the two options.

You will also know that for this trade, there are two break-even points because it is possible for the trade to earn profits no matter which way the market goes. The upper break-even point will be 8770 and the lower break-even point was 8280.

Below is the profit loss payoff diagram. It is going to show the profit and the loss that is plotted against the various expiry prices for the stock that you choose.

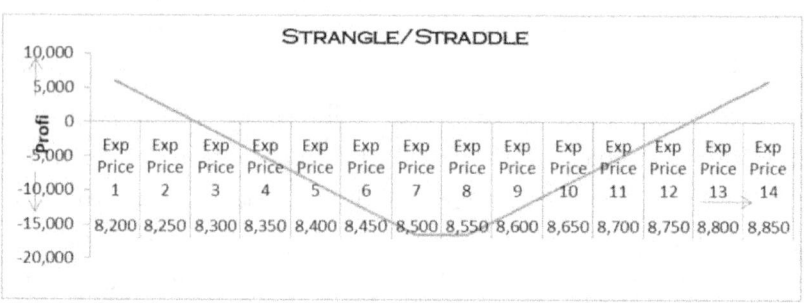

Now let's take a look at the results that the trader was able to get from these trades. This trade was held for three days. Then on the 11th of November, once the election votes were counted in the United States and the Republicans won, the stock market in India reacted negatively and the chosen index fell by more than 300 points. Because of this sharp fall, the Nifty index, thanks to the long straddle, feel into high profits. Both of your positions ended up squaring off back to back before the trading day closed and the profits were booked.

However, it is important to know exactly when to get out of the market with this kind of trade. While the market quickly went down right after the election results were posted, this negative sentiment only lasted for a day and it did not take long for the market to swing back up the next day. If the trader had stayed in the market for another day, the upswing in the market would have meant they would have lost all of their money. The volatility drop ad the time decay issue would have made it so that the trader would lose out. But they got out of the market at the right time and they made a good amount of profit.

The total amount that the trader decided to spend on this investment for both of the positions ended up being 16,500. In the end, they made a net profit of 11,250. This means that they made a return on investment of 68 percent in just three days.

While this one had a big return on investment, you have to be careful with the volatility and you have to know when to get out of the market. If the trader had stayed in the market for a little bit longer, they would have lost a lot of their money instead of getting a profit in the process. These markets are hard to work with because they go up and down so quickly, but if you are able to guess the right time to get out and you pick the right strike prices, you can make unlimited profits in the process.

Protective Collar

The protective collar strategy is when an investor buys a put option that is out-of-the-money and then writes an out-of-the-money call option on the same asset with the same expiration date. The strategy can be conceived primarily as an exit strategy because it is usually written by traders who have been with a stock for a long while. The stock has performed well, and they are looking to protect their investment in case the price falls or rises surprisingly.

So take the Lemonade Inc. shares. There has been an announcement on an exciting new product called the sugar-free lemonade slushy. The company is convinced that with the growing movement in society towards healthy habits, the new product will pick up and might even find its way into state schools without much resistance. So big sales are expected from this. You own Lemonade Inc. stock, a hundred shares now valued at $100 per share. The announcement causes a spike in the price.

Over the next few months, the company is doing well, especially over the summer months and autumn. But with winter approaching, they might start to see sales dwindle.

Your shares have appreciated by a tremendous amount to $170 per share. You can hop off now, and you would have made a profit of $7,000 from your starting point. The thing is, you hear rumors of Lemonade Inc. launching a new product that might do well in the winter. But this very product might hurt them and see those facing fierce competitors on the market. So you are in a position where if there is some gain, despite how weak that rise is, you want to profit off it, but if the plan backfires, you would like to exit with the profit you have already made.

To achieve this, you would implement a protective collar.

You would write a call option at a $175 strike price at $2 per share. Then you would go on and purchase a put option at the strike price of $168 at $2 per share. In this situation, if the price of Lemonade Inc. drops below $168, you would be in a position to cash out by selling your stock at $168 per share.

If Lemonade Inc.'s price rises above $175, you would sell that stock at $175 and earn a profit from the rise in stock price. Since you have paid $2 per contract on your put options and received the same amount for the call option you sold, you now have paid virtually nothing for the protection you get from using this move because the two transactions cancel each other out.

However, this is not always the case. All protective collar strategies will be different depending on the options prices, but showing it is possible is encouraging enough.

The Iron Condor

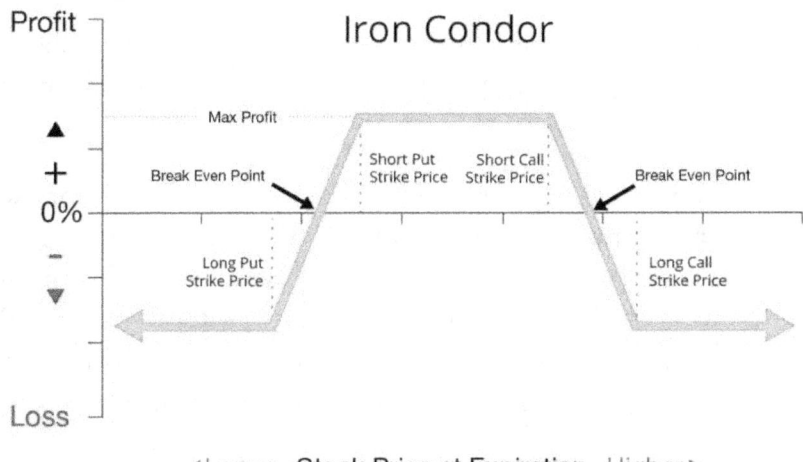

The other strategy that we talked about was directional strategies, but the iron condor is going to be a non-directional strategy. This one is going to limit your profit a bit but its probability of success is pretty high for the traders that are able to trade it well. When you are working with an Iron Condor trade, no matter which way the stock or the index ends up moving, the trader is going to become profitable as long as the movement stays inside the boundaries that the trader sets, at the time of expiry. Out of all the strategies that we are going to discuss in this guidebook, this one has the highest potential to give you profits and it has the least amount of risk as well.

You will use the iron condor to trade on stocks with very low volatility. It is not a good idea to go with a stock that moves around quite a bit and has big highs and lows that go all over the place. You will find that this is a credit spread strategy that will be viewed as a combination of the bear call spread (which we talk about in the following chapter) and the bull put spread.

You can consider the iron condor as a type of evergreen strategy, one that a lot of traders are going to use when they find a stable stock. As a trader, if you are able to choose any strategy and you want to go with one that is pretty easy to follow and will give you a higher probability of doing well, then the iron condor is the best option for you to choose.

The iron condor is going to be a little bit more difficult to work with because there are four legs to go with it, rather than the two legs on the other trading strategy. For the first step, you need to go through and find the stock that you would like to work with. Remember that for the iron condor to work, you need to have a stock that is pretty stable and is not going to go up or down too much in the process.

The next step is to sell one deep OTM put option of the stock that you selected. Then buy one OTM put options with the same expiry date and with the same stock that you sold in the first step, but make sure that this one has a lower strike price.

After those steps are done, it is time to sell again. This time you are going to sell a deep OTM, but it needs to be a call option. You want this to use the same stock and have the same expiry date as what you used in the last part. And finally, you can buy an OTM call option that has the same stock and the same expiry date as all the other steps, but this one needs to have a slightly higher strike-price.

One thing to note is that there is going to be a difference between the strike prices the two put options need to be the same as the difference between the strikes of the two call options if you want to create this strategy accurately. Throughout the time until the expiry, you will want to monitor how your position is doing. Unless you are certain that your stock is going to keep within the limits that you have placed, you will want to consider exiting out of the trade when the position is making 50% or more of the maximum profit that you want out of this trade. If you find that the market goes against your expectations and there is a big directional movement of your stock, it is time to close out all of the positions and wait until that stock has time to stabilize before entering again.

You would choose to go with this strategy any time that your stock is showing a really low amount of volatility. This means that the stock is not moving much or if it is moving within a range that you are able to define easily. For the most part, index options are going to be the best for executing this strategy compared to stock-based options since these indexes are often less volatile. If you are working with a market that is pretty stable, you will find that iron condors are the safest option for winning.

The biggest advantage of using the iron condor is that it is considered a neutral position and you are likely to get some kind of profit as long as you execute this strategy the right way, no matter which way your chosen stock or index ends up moving. And since this is a net credit strategy, it will be able to help you work against the issues with time decay.

The biggest disadvantage that you are going to find with the iron condor is that the returns that you will get out of it are quite a bit less than what you can get from a directional strategy. In addition, the maximum loss that you can incur is going to be quite a bit more than the maximum profit that you would be able to gain in this position if you are not careful with the stocks that you are using. However, when looking at the statistics for success with the iron condor, you will notice that the probability of a win is going to be much higher than that of a loss, which helps to make this a great strategy to work with.

Now it is time to take a look at an example of when the iron condor trade can be successful. For this one, we are going to enter into the trade on the 17th of April and the underlying index that is used is the Nifty 50. This is considered a benchmark index of the National Stock Exchange in India. This is a good one to use with the iron condor because it has a history of stability and doesn't usually move up and down too much.

The reason that we are entering with this strategy is because the Nifty index has just reached a 52-week high and there has been some profit booking. Since that time, it has been trading in a narrow range showing that there is some support for it staying around 9100 and when it reaches 9300, there seems to be some strong resistance. When looking at the near future, it isn't expected that there are going to be some big triggers that would cause a big rise or drop in the price and when looking at the history of the index, it usually doesn't go up or down more than three percent on average through the money.

This means over the next month, it is not likely that the index is not going to go higher than the 9500, and it is not likely that it will fall below 8900 within the next month. This helps them to make the conditions perfect to work with the iron condor.

The first step that you need to take when working on an iron condor trade is to pick out your stock. You want one that doesn't have a lot of movement or at least one that has predictable movement between the same two points. Some of the things that you should also consider when it comes to using the iron condor strategy includes: All of the options that you pick should have a minimum of 30 days to expiry so that enough premium can be collected. Because of this, this case study picked an expiry date that was 38 days in the future, so the 25**th** of May.

The trade needs to have a high probability of success, at least 70 percent. To make sure that this happens, the 8900 Nifty put option and then the 9500-call option were the points that are chosen. Since this stock has only recently fixed itself and was currency near the 9150 mark, the strikes that were chosen for the call gave some extra room because it was more likely that the index would increase rather than decrease.

The second thing that you should do is sell one deep OTM put option. The 8900 Nifty put option that expired in May was sold for 42.25. You need to buy an OTM put option that has a lower strike price than your sold option. For this example, we used the 8700 put option, gave it a May expiry, and then bought it for 19.70.

Now you need to work on the next leg. This one is going to ask you to sell a deep OTM call option. In this example, we bought a 9500-call option that would expire in May and we sold it for 23. And finally, you also need to purchase an OTM call option. We bought a 9700-call option for 4.85.

Based on the prices that were present on the individual legs of the positions we chose, the maximum potential profit that can be made will be 3278 and the maximum potential loss that you could get if the stock doesn't go the way that you would like, would be 11,723.

Summary Table		
Stock or Index Traded	Nifty	
Lot size for each option	75	
Option 1	Strike Price	8,700.00
Lower-strike Put Option - Buy	Premium Paid	19.70
Option 2	Strike Price	8,900.00
Higher-strike Put Option - Sell	Premium Received	45.25
Option 3	Strike Price	9,500.00
Lower-strike Call Option - Sell	Premium Received	23.00
Option 4	Strike Price	9,700.00
Higher-strike Call Option - Buy	Premium Paid	4.85
Difference Between any 2 Consecutive Strikes-prices		50.00
Max Profit		₹ 3,278
Max Loss		₹ -11,723
Condition for meeting max profit	Stock price at expiry lies between Strike-Prices of Option 2 and Option 3	
Condition for meeting max loss	Stock Price at expiry > Strike-price of Option4 -OR- Stock Price at expiry < Strike-price of Option 1	
Upper Break-even Price at Expiry	Stock/Index at time of expiry =	9,543.70
Lower Break-even Price at Expiry	Stock/Index at time of expiry =	8,856.30

Remember that with the iron condor strategy, there are going to be two points that are the break-even point. The upper one is going to be at 9543.7, and the lower one is going to be 8856.2. The profit and loss diagram below are going to show the profit and loss that you can get based on the different expiry prices for this stock during this trade.

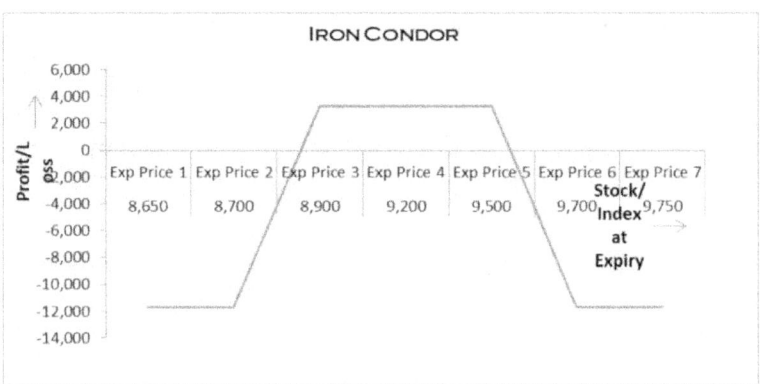

With this example, the position was held for three weeks before the trader closed it. The trader technically had two weeks in order to keep the stocks going before they hit their expiry, but in this case, the trader wanted to be able to exit the trade and free up their capital to work on another trade. In addition, this stock had started to climb up to a new high, and there was the possibility that this momentum was going to keep going up, and the trader may have lost all of their profit.

During these three weeks, the stock ended up gaining 250 points. Despite this, this trade still provided a profit of thirty percent of the maximum potential profit thanks to the time-day, and because of the time exit. The trader was still about to earn 1024 from this trade.

The return of investment on this option was lower. The trader was about to earn about 1.25 percent on their return on investment. Usually, the iron condor strategy is going to be more effective than this when it comes to a good return on investment, but during the time of the trade, the stock ended up moving more than was expected. A similar trade using this stock usually will give at least three percent return on investment, but the market was not as steady as it usually is. But the trader decided to get out of the market ahead of time to make sure that the market didn't go outside of their limits and make them lose money in the process.

Iron Butterfly

An iron butterfly is another strategy to use if you think the stock price will stay within a certain range. It will use four options, like the iron condor, but there will be three different strike prices.

In this case, you will sell a put option and a call option with the same strike price. The strategy is to get as close to at the money as possible. We will call the strike priced used the central strike. Then you set a differential price we will call x. Now you buy a put option with a strike price of (central strike $- x$), and you buy a call option with a strike price of (central strike $+ x$).

Like an iron condor, the profit from an iron butterfly is fixed at the net credit when you sell to open. This is given by the sum of the premiums earned from selling the at the money call and put, minus the prices paid for the out of the money options.

The maximum loss is the strike price of the purchased call − strike price of the sold put − total premium.

CHAPTER 5:

OPTION TRADING AND STOCK TRADING

Why use stock market strategies?

Here is a good question. Why is it worth using stock market strategies? You need to know that the financial instruments you are trading on, such as CFDs (contracts for difference), are already designed to be simplified and accessible for investment.

Even the platforms where you will find yourself performing from a practical point of view, your trading operations are very intuitive and can, therefore, be exploited both by industry experts who demand the possibility of trading professionally, via beginners who may never have put to this kind of tools but still want to create a monthly income by investing in the stock market.

One of the right reasons why it is worth learning the stock market strategies lies in the fact that we are sure that you too have always dreamed of finding a job that would not force you to move for long stretches, perhaps remaining stuck in traffic and city chaos, a job that does not oblige you to say yes to the boss on duty who may not even deserve to occupy that place, a job where you should not be forced to work overtime to be able to reach the end of the month charging you with stress and fatigue.

This is why we believe that trading with stock market strategies is the best possible alternative, not only offline but also online. Being independent in this promising world guarantees you the possibility to shake off the problems linked to the crisis to earn your freedom, even before the money, to become the master of your own life.

A thousand good reasons to trade with the right strategy

If you find yourself somehow, you have heard about the possibility of trading on the stock exchange, and maybe you know there is no way to do it online. If you want to take this path, we ask you not to feel intimidated or frightened by your possible future as a financial operator.

The stock exchange trading online has become a beginner or beginner's measure that it is. If, until today, you have only played lowly professions and do not have a higher degree, perhaps you think that you are not up to this kind of activity.

Perhaps you believe that the Stock Exchange and Markets, as well as the strategies to earn money, are beyond your means! Enough of this loser mentality.

The truth is that you are second to none, and you have the potential to be on a par with others and, why not, also to excel, especially in a world where meritocracy reigns like that of the stock market and financial markets on the internet.

Millions of people around the world have chosen the path of investment of their online capital, albeit very small. Now you can do it yourself by putting into practice the stock market strategies that we will propose to you during this guide.

Anyone who makes money from online trading does so from little to useful knowledge. It is, therefore, not a question of quantity; it is only a question of quality.

Few but good stock market strategies will allow you to become an established and successful trader who can afford to buy whatever he wants, in total independence, and without having to ask anyone for anything.

It is necessary to know as well as to apply the right bag technique. Learn it first through theory, then put it into practice in the field of trading, testing it continuously and optimizing it based on your trading methodology.

Do not miss the topics to come and immediately discover the best stock exchange strategies, the path that will lead you to become a real trader may be extended and tortuous, but in the end it will be worth it, and you will finally feel satisfied in an occupation free from conditioning and the harassment of the world of work as it has always known it.

If you start trading today, your old life will already be in the past because you're about to be immersed in a virtuous circle of real opportunities to become an ace of stock trading. Cheers!

Modern stock exchange strategies have been devised to permanently change the old canons of traditional investment that made everything too slow and stiff, too challenging to apply, and this caused traders many problems and dissatisfactions, so much that many were eventually led to abandon this promising activity.

With the new strategies, the goal has been to make trading affordable and feasible for everyone, the doors are wide open, and anyone who wants it today can enter without suffering the typical problems of the past.

What it takes to make the most of the strategies that we propose to you in all respects is only basic knowledge of the subject of trading. Consequently, you are not called to know everything to start earning.

Therefore, trading does not mean having a degree in economics. After all, those who would be prepared today to face 5 years of studies to earn money, it is really too much time and too much sacrifice to put in place, so the techniques that you have to use to earn are simple but effective strategies that guarantee the success of the trades in most cases.

But because in stock trading, we talk about strategies and not tactics and because the former is much more successful and secure than the latter. The speech is very simple, and we want to clarify it with the following short definitions:

Investment Strategies

The strategy is the description of a long-term action plan used to set and subsequently coordinate all the actions that serve to achieve a particular, specific purpose. Strategies can be applied in all fields to reach the goal.

Therefore, they carry out the task of obtaining greater security by making a series of separate operations that help reach an end goal. In the case of trading, we are talking about profit, which is undoubtedly the only primary aim that drives people to enter this business.

The simple tactic, on the other hand, is a course of action adopted according to the achievement of specific objectives, but in this case, we speak of small achievements in the short-term.

Adopting tactics would not be effective or satisfactory in the field of trading because it is not a structured plan, but simple plans to achieve small temporary objectives. In short, with a tactic, you can also win a battle, but not war; winning a war requires a broader STRATEGY.

What all traders aim to achieve is a constant and lasting success over time that gives total security of a monthly income and specific collections on an annual basis. In stock exchange trading, it is possible to achieve all this by using strategies. Without strategies, you might perish as a trader very soon.

Applying stock exchange strategies requires attention and many precautions, especially at the beginning, when you are not much of an expert. In certain situations, when the markets become uncertain or careless, you do not know how to act, and you risk making mistakes.

At specific errors, however, the strategies cannot be remedied; in those cases, it will be the experience to act as a master and to suggest the right moves to make.

How much do you earn if you use the best strategy to invest?

With financial instruments available today, profit margins are simply impressive; operating in the right way, you can earn a lot of money even on a daily basis, but at that point, you have to take into account other factors such as the skill of the trader, the ability to avoid the losses, the amount of capital you have available, but also the small strokes of luck that from time to time can help to increase profits.

The amount of money that can be earned then also depends, above all, on the financial product you intend to use. There are not very marked differences but still tangible, depending on whether you prefer to trade forex, CFD, or investing in social trading.

Stock Market Strategies and Money Management

If you intend to trade on the stock exchange, there is no doubt that you will, sooner or later, have to come into contact with the rules of money management or all that concerns the management of money and your precious investment capital.

Money Management shows you the way to correct money management, so it is fundamental in trading, but its rules are also applied in other fields that are as varied as in the domestic or business economy. Ultimately, the rules it dictates are quite simple and due to pure and simple common sense, but in any case, it will be necessary to observe them religiously to avoid running into severe problems in your career as a trader.

The creators of the first money management techniques had a clear idea that it was necessary to produce a new awareness of the use of money in their investments, for the first time imposing the concept of diversification and differentiation of the investment portfolio to reduce the risks of trading and losses on investment capital drastically.

A strategic approach to stock exchange trading cannot, therefore, ignore the knowledge of the fundamental precepts of money management that require you to always establish the spending limit and the budget available at the beginning.

In the field of trading, this will mean establishing the risks that you are willing to run within certain limits that not even an "Indiana Jones" of trading could ever think of crossing; otherwise, it would face economic suicide at the speed of light! The principles of money management help you put both the risks and the potential profits on the scales to understand if a particular movement on the markets should be exploited or not; in other words, it helps you to know if the game is worth the candle.

If you learn to put the rules of money management into practice, your long-term success can be practically assured, but even the short and medium-term will be more probable and easily accessible. In short, all this talk turns to a need for investment efficiency.

The best traders are those who can minimize losses, which not even the guru of the economy could ever avoid and increase profits more and more.

The key to all this is precisely the fact that before learning to earn aspiring traders, the importance of learning to lose should be taught! Suffering losses and spilling money is a natural thing in trading, and you have to try to understand it and not give too much weight when a loss occurs.

The main rule of money management states that you should never, never, ever put at risk more than 5% of the total capital available in a single trading operation.

Doing so would be stupid because it means that in case of loss, you should lose a lot of time trying to recover the negative position if you succeed. Furthermore, it is necessary to avoid losing more than 30% of the total capital available in a single trading day.

You simply have to recognize that when a bad day happens, you have to have the courage to turn off the computer or the device that you used to use to go for a nice walk and not run any further risk because it is clear that that day or you are not able to operate correctly or things in some way always row against you. It is the case to abandon the current session as soon as possible.

Guide to Investing in Stocks

Without a proper guide, all that information you have gained from reading through this instructive book would be for nothing. In this chapter, we will compress and expand on all the investment guidelines hinted at in earlier topics and provide you with an authoritative and practical guide to investing in stocks—the things you need to keep in mind and the exact order of actions that any investor hoping to establish themselves in the stock market ought to follow.

What comes first? What follows that first action? The activities described here are ordered as they are for maximum efficiency. They comprise of a three-step process that starts with the preparations you need to make before starting your investment journey, followed by the actual investment procedure, and ending with the follow-up activities you need to do to ensure that your investment flourishes. Thus ordered, it makes up for a complete guide to investing in stocks aimed at setting you off on your investment journey with the proper skills and capabilities to ensure profitability in the long run.

Laying the Groundwork

Before you start investing, it is important that you define your objectives and investment goals based on your current capital endowment. From there, you will then decide what style of investing best suits you. To make both of these decisions, you will need to build your knowledge bank.

Build Your Knowledge Bank

A wise investor is a wealthy investor. Knowledge is the most important asset an investor accumulates before putting down the money for their first investment. Good investment strategizing comes from having a good grasp of not just financial markets and what sends prices rising and dropping; it also requires that you have a proper understanding of investment strategies and all assets available for you to invest in. Lack of knowledge in the ins and outs of the stock market can have a debilitating effect on an investor. On the other hand, sufficient information, even when it is just theoretical, is a huge boost of confidence. Investors who have a good idea of how people make money in the stock market are more likely to succeed in the stock market themselves because they are exposed to all the strategies that others before them have accumulated.

On the other hand, acquiring even a rudimentary cache of knowledge of investing is assured to put you way ahead of contemporary investors who just put their money in the so-called "hottest" stocks. And the good thing about knowledge acquisition is that it comes in handy whether you are starting your investment journey at the age of 26 or 62. The deeper you go in your learning of the ropes, the more chances you stand for becoming an outstanding investor.

To build your knowledge bank, you will need to gather information from research, reading financial books, observing the masters of the game, and following the market very keenly.

Learn Research Skills

The first rule of investing in stocks is to invest only in companies that you understand. You will need thorough research to understand the current state of the stock market, rising trends, and future projections. Research skills are crucial not just to the actions you will carry out in this practical guide but also later in your investment journey as you pick assets to buy and determine the best buying and selling points for each one of them.

By learning to research, you unlock every successful investor's catalog of investing stratagems and tricks. Research skills are very handy as you lay the groundwork for your investment journey, when you start the real process of investing, and afterward, as you keep your portfolio balanced. In the preliminary process, your research skills will help you to learn, among other things, what information is needed to become a good investor. As you select the stockbrokers with whom to open a brokerage account, research skills will also be very handy. You will also need to have polished research skills as you conduct the due diligence analysis of prospective stocks and other assets to put in your stock portfolio.

The good thing about having technology in our hands is that research skills often entail a simple Google search and bookmarking a few articles for later reference. But people often neglect even the simple act of reading the Wikipedia article of the company they are thinking about buying stocks in. As a tip for those exhaustive online searches, use a PC if one is handy. Some of the most informative articles you will find about a critical topic will never make it into the search results of your mobile phone browser.

Read

Reading investment books may be the hardest method of adding to your knowledge bank. But the information that you gather from investment books goes a long way in building your investment skills. Books written by investment legends (a biography, for example) would be especially indispensable because investors will usually share information about their own investment journey, including the mistakes they made along the way. You can then avoid these mistakes in your own investment career and possibly save yourself a fortune.

Books actually make up for a short course you take on whatever topic they are about, giving you comprehensive information on various subtopics. And neither should your readership be limited to books written about the financial markets specifically. Read up, too, on other skills that could come in handy in your portfolio management, such as accounting and bookkeeping. These skills come in handy in the investment process as well as out of it—other areas of your life.

Deciding on how to invest in stocks

There are numerous ways on how to invest in stocks. All of these ways have some advantages and disadvantages, but every individual's situation is different. What's good for you may lead to a problematic situation for another. Considering the period and market value, while looking for stocks to invest in, is highly recommended.

Sometimes, the market may be going through a smooth and steady path that your emotional aspects may get in the way. You may invest in expensive stocks due to the success of the market. On the other hand, in a poorly performing market during situations like inflation, you may start to sell off your stocks.

So how can you decide where to invest? First off, you need to analyze how much a certain method of investment would be affected by the level of risk and potential loses. If the risk is too high, but the gains from it would be more fruitful, you would know what step to take. Such decision making requires proper research of all the methods and a proper understanding of how much would be at stake, in different situations.

Methods of investment

We know that all methods would have certain effects, but in the end, the success relies on how much risk you are ready to take, as well as how much knowledge you have in stock marketing. If you're into a more modern and technological way of business, then you should know, online buying of stocks is a thing. However, it is only recommended if you are well aware of how the stock market operates, and can give useful advice to yourself, as this one doesn't involve any advices to be given, so you're on your own. Also, it is far more risky, as you are charged only a flat fee for each transaction. Also, to mention, it's time-consuming, as you would have to train yourself until you're confident enough to take the next step.

Investment Club

The next method which you can consider is through the investment clubs. You meet a lot of people who may be going through the same situation you are, and people who can give professional and financial advices. Other people's experiences can make you learn a lot too. It is affordable and can help you to understand and differentiate between different market situations. Increased involvement and investing in stocks through this can help you gain a new perspective and a sense of direction.

Full-Service Broker

Then we have a full-service broker. Know that this is an expensive method, as the fees paid to your broker I quite high, but the excess information makes up for it.

The broker will help you with the recommendation and advice on how to take the next step, and the precaution measure to be taken while looking for a good financial advisor. This leads to increased business know-how, more knowledge about the stock market, and increased confidence in your decisions.

Investing in the stock markets

If you purchase some clothes and neglect the fact that trying it on would help you decide whether to purchase it or not and come home to only find out that the clothes don't fit, you'll be pretty disappointed unless there is an exchange or return policy at the outlet. If not, you're at a loss. Trust me, investing in a market is nothing close to purchasing clothes. Hence, neglecting can lead to the loss of a fortune. Louder for the people at the back, investing in stock markets is nothing close to your day to day spending. So, you got to go smart about it.

Investing in stocks for the first time has a much greater risk. However, these risks are to be taken, but there is always supposed to be a margin. The potential risk always needs to be managed. How do you ask? Research gets you a long way. You don't want to trust the company blindly. It is important to analyze and study how the company is doing in the market. Their marketing tactics, financial weaknesses, and productivity need to be kept in mind.

If the business doesn't have a good marketing department, it's likely to go crashing down as soon as the competition gets tough. The finance department needs to be checked and observed at every point, as they handle a major part of the business. Any fishy business being done, the greater is the effect on you. Whatever the business is selling, it needs to have a good production plan, method, and a skilled and efficient workforce.

The trends in the market should be considered at all points

Consumer taste and changes in choices should be properly analyzed, and the reasons behind them should be known. If the owners of the business have enough knowledge about this, and the managers are efficient enough to make this happen, it means your potential risk may be lower.

As a beginner, what is important to take into account, is how the country's economy is doing. Inflation would mean that there can be a sudden downfall in the trends and a greater risk of bankruptcy. The time of investing should be carefully chosen. However, it is proven that there never is the perfect time to invest in the market. Comparison of different timings is important. This also depends on the type of goods or services being offered. The price elasticity of demand and supply would help you find out how the market will do during inflation.

Moreover, for long term success, the growth of the company needs to be taken into consideration. Over time, how much the company has actually grown, and what is the difference between its earnings when it started fresh, and what is it now? This determines the stability of the company you plan to invest in. Many businesses go through ups and downs, but the major ones are what you should avoid at all cost. The strength of the industry and how well it does in the market will show how much potential the company has for long-term success.

Coming on to the other important aspects, the debt and the equity ratio needs to be measured beforehand. If the company is in too much debt and isn't making enough profit to pay it off, it would call for the liquidation, which means selling off the assets of the company. You won't be left with anything in this case.

Learn to Follow the Market

When buying assets for your investment portfolio, timing the market is one of the most futile things you can ever do. But in building your knowledge bank, analyzing the market comes in very handy when analyzing how the stock market reacts to different stimuli. Following the market improves your understanding of it because, after all, observation is one of the most useful skills in building knowledge.

Financial news services, such as the Wall Street Journal, Bloomberg, Yahoo! Finance, and Morningstar, among numerous others, are practically indispensable for a new investor hoping to understand the stock market. You will be able to identify the most profitable sectors of the economy, making it easier for you to make the decision on what stocks to buy when it finally comes down to it. Following the market is the only way to identify trends as they form, stay updated on emerging business concepts, and learn more about general business practices and their impact on profitability.

Television is another great way to broaden your knowledge base. Apart from the jargon (which is also good to learn), analysts on TV teach you how to anticipate market reaction to geopolitical, economic, and public relations events. Of course, at some point, you will outgrow the rather shallow and junky analysis, but in the beginning, they could be a treasure trove of information.

Define Your Investment Style

After building your knowledge bank substantially and gaining a deeper understanding of the stock market in general, it is time now to narrow the focus down to your own investment. Everyone has the style of investing that best suits their needs and their personality. Risk-takers need an investment strategy quite different from risk-averse people, and those who treasure balance would like to combine aspects of both. In this step of your investment journey, you start thinking more about the exact ways that you are going to invest.

Vision Statement

A vision statement gives you the chance to define exactly what you are looking to achieve in monetary rewards. The rest of your investment journey is reliant on your ability to define your investment vision statement because this is the point where you factor in your goals (reasons for saving up through investment) and plot out the best route to follow to get there faster and with minimal risk. When defining your vision statement, establish exactly how much money you are looking to have at the end of your investment and how much time you have to raise it. From this assessment, you can determine the kind of investment strategy that will enable you to achieve your goal.

A popular vision for investing is the 25× goal, a dividend stock-investment strategy for people with visions of early retirement that stipulates that you should invest in stocks that pay you enough dividends to match your annual salary. So, assuming that the stocks in your investment portfolio give a dividend payout of about 4% and with $50,000 as your annual salary, you'd need to invest 25 times of that, which comes to $1.25 million to make exactly what you make now. All dividends and any additional savings go toward boosting your investment portfolio, buying more dividend stocks to increase the dividend payout, which is then reinvested for even greater yields.

Factoring in any possible future promotions (and the accompanying raise) and rising expenditures as you accumulate more responsibilities and develop more refined tastes, $50,000 a year will probably be too little twenty years from now. You will probably need $60,000–75,000 to maintain your current lifestyle, adjusting for inflation. You can solve for that discrepancy easily. Just factor in the desired annual dividend payout, calculate with the average yield and find out how much more you will need to have invested. The best thing about the 25× goal idea is that even when you finally start living off your investment, it will still leave your principal intact.

Investment Strategy

With the overarching determinant being your investment goals, your investment strategy is influenced by two main factors—the amount of risk you think you can shoulder and the kind of investor you would like to become in terms of active participation.

Based on risk tolerance, you can be a conservative investor, an aggressive one, or a moderate one. Aggressive investing produces massive profits very fast, and it is suitable for investors with huge goals and a short period of time to pursue them. The risks are rather massive, but then so are the rewards. Conservative investors opt for low-yield investments that are low in risk. Even though this strategy could be quite profitable over the long term, it could also make your investment a very unprofitable venture. Going for the most conservative investment opportunities also means that the chances of missing out on amazing investment opportunities also increase substantially. The balanced strategy is for those investors who want the best of both worlds—medium returns at average risk.

Based on participation, you can either be a passive investor or an active one. A passive investor invests and forgets all about the investment. They don't bother much with price fluctuations and such "trivial" matters. If you want to have the confidence to invest in a stock and forget about it (watch the money flow, as it were), then make *thorough background research* your friend. This way, you won't be worried that your portfolio is losing value because of a stock you picked. Active investors are a whole other breed altogether. More suited to day trading than long-term investments, active portfolio management nonetheless produces great profits.

Investment strategies ultimately come down to the choice of assets that an investor puts in their portfolio. Aggressive investment strategies call for massive growth stocks with high risks and price volatility, a balanced approach seeks out medium growth rate stocks, while conservative investors prefer the tried and tested stocks whose core business faces absolutely no risk of collapse. Active stock investing gravitates more toward the aggressive style, while conservative investing is often passive. Conservative stocks tend to belong to old companies that have established themselves. The opposite is true for aggressive stocks, whose companies are much younger and require a steady hand to halt any possible loss of investment from price volatility.

Having established your priorities and set your investment goals and strategies, it is high time you open an account and get down to the real investing. It is during this phase that you will pick the asset that will go into your investment portfolio. But first, you will need to open a brokerage account.

Open a Brokerage Account

To invest in the financial markets, you are going to need a broker to carry out your buy and sell orders. You should be very careful when picking out your brokerage because even though their only job is to facilitate your investments in stocks, bonds, investment trusts, and the money markets, not all brokers are created equal. There are those that facilitate your investment and do nothing more (discount brokers), and then you have the ones that throw in some sound investing advice into the deal (full-service brokers). A rising trend in brokerage account holding is the robo-advisor type of account where an automated system helps you set goals, buy stocks, and transact. Your choice of brokerage account will be determined by the amount of control you desire.

Discount Brokerage Accounts

Discount brokers carry out your buy/sell orders at a very low price. A discount brokerage account is the ultimate do-it-yourself investment account. Other than some basic information and price comparison tools, discount brokers offer investors virtually no guidance on investment strategizing, whether in the preliminary stages or later on as you manage your investment portfolio. The discount broker is a relatively recent development in the stock market. Previously, only the full-service broker existed, serving the rich because only they (with their deep pockets and huge investments) can afford their services. The discount broker opened up the stock market for people with less capital to participate.

One of the most outstanding discount brokerage accounts is TD Ameritrade. The firm offers great price comparison and analysis tools. Even though you will get no real investment guidance from a person sitting across the desk or on the other side of the phone, with TD Ameritrade, there will be enough information that you may not need an advisor anyways. If you created a good investment objective and came up with the correct strategy, then you probably won't miss these services anyway.

Full-Service Brokers

A full-service brokerage account entails more than the execution of just buy/sell orders. A wide variety of services, such as taxation advice, research tools, financial guidance, and retirement planning, are offered along with the usual execution of your buy and sell orders. The commission charged by full-service brokers eclipses that of discount ones a few times over. The advantage is that you need not get tied up with research, stock selection, and portfolio management.

Because full-service brokers tend to be more traditional and well-established, they tend to have a few benefits that discount brokers don't. For one thing, a full-service brokerage firm is more likely to have a direct link to IPOs, preferred stocks, and other glamorous opportunities. In the same manner, they tend to put together their own investment products, such as ETFs and mutual funds, giving investors an even wider range of investment opportunities to take advantage of.

Robo-advisor Accounts

The robo-advisor brokerage account is the rave in discount stock trading right now. In a few short steps, robo-advisors allow you to create a portfolio of diverse investments and manage these investment opportunities. Robo-advisors use technology to bring together the best features from full-service and discount brokerage to create an outstanding investment vehicle for the average investor. With little more than your personal details, investment goal, and risk tolerance, a robo-advisor creates a portfolio for you and administers it, performing such mundane tasks as rebalancing with little input from you. Keep updating the details and objectives to ensure that the account still reflects your needs. Other than that, investing using a rob-advisor is a pretty hands-off approach to investing.

Even though robo-advisors do not offer the deep house services of full-service brokerage firms, such as special investment opportunities, the wealth management tools are right up there with the best. The three features that make a robo-advisor account such an attractive opportunity for an investor include (1) low upfront investment, (2) great options, and (3) inclusive portfolio management. Moreover, robo-advisors are completely unbiased, making recommendations based solely on your investment goals. The conflict of interest that comes from financial advisors pushing preferential investments to their clients is totally eliminated. The requirements to open a robo-advisor account are also pretty relaxed, which means that you can start investing with as low as $500. Numerous robo-advisor account providers have come up in the past one decade or so, including Betterment, Schwab Intelligent Portfolios, Wealthfront, and SigFig, among numerous others.

With a brokerage account open, the only thing left to do is pick your investments. The options available to you include the 401(k) plan, the individual retirement plan (IRA), and of course, the stocks, bonds, and other assets that you can invest through a brokerage account.

401(K) and IRA Plans

The 401(k) plan is every employee's birthright to the world of investment. It allows you to save for your employment in the most productive way possible—with incremental returns. The contributions to the investment portfolio are also automatic and tax-deductible. A clause stipulating exactly when you will receive full access to your funds is another advantage of 401(k) plans—it allows you to plan for your own investment.

Whatever amount you decide to contribute to your 401(k) plan is taken out of your pay slip before you get the money, which means that your taxable income reduces substantially. As an investment that matures upon retirement, a 401(k) comes in very handy in addition to any other personal investment plan you may have going if your goal is to retire early, like if your investment vision is based on the 25× goal.

An IRA plan allows you to save for huge future cash expenditures, such as retirement, house buying, a car, college fees, *etc.* There are a few versions of the IRA plan available, including the traditional, Roth, SIMPLE, and SEP versions.

CHAPTER 6:

TAKE CONTROL OF YOUR MONEY

Money & Risk Management Techniques

For successful trading in the stock markets, money management and risk management are crucial steps. Stock markets can turn highly volatile at times, and if you are not careful about protecting your money and risk of open trades, you can suffer huge monetary losses.

Therefore, the first step in day trading should be; learn how to reduce trading risk and manage your capital investment so you can tolerate the normal losses in day trading. Money management is like strengthening your defenses so you can survive in the stock market to trade another day. Safe trading practices to protect your money can increase your profits. A lack of it can also double your losses. Money and risk management can be the difference between the success and failure of a day trader. Often, beginners are so focused on making profits in stock markets, they forget to protect their invested capital, and soon, their losses wipe out the whole trading capital.

Part of good money management is using just a fraction of your trading capital on one trade. In other words, never put all your money on a single trade. As they say, 90% of traders do not make profits in day trading. A big reason for this failure is not paying attention to money management. If you keep on betting on stock prices for rising of falling with no proper strategy and risk management, then it is pure gambling and not any intelligent business venture.

Take day trading as a business, do it with proper money management, learn how you can reduce the risk in your trades; you will reduce the number of potential losses, and increase potential profits. Keep your trading cost to a minimum. Before opening any trade, always decide how much loss you will allow for that trade and put a stop loss to cover that much amount. Markets will come back the next day, but you should be left with enough capital to trade when markets open for the next session.

Risk Management

Risk management is one of the most important parts of option trading. Like with any other kind of investment, trading is inherently risky. There will always be some amount of risk involved, but the key to trading successfully is to manage your capital and risk carefully.

Everyone has a different risk tolerance threshold, and that's completely fine. You should never stretch yourself too thin. Only trade with money you can afford to lose. Let's look at some ways you can control and manage your risk efficiently.

When people think of day trading, they only think of potential profits, not losses. Therefore, day trading attracts so many people that don't see the risk of losses. In stock markets, various events can trigger losses for investors and traders, which are beyond their control. These events can be economic conditions such as recession, geopolitical changes, also, changes in the central bank policies, natural disasters, or sometimes terror attacks.

This is the market risk; the potential of losing money due to unknown and sudden factors. These factors affect the overall performance of stock markets, and regardless of how careful one is while day trading, the possibility of market risk is always present, which can cause losses. The market risk is known as the systematic risk because it influences the entire stock market. There is also a nonsystematic risk, which affects only a specific industry or company. Long-term investors tackle this risk by diversification in their investment portfolio.

Unlike investors, day traders have no method to neutralize market risk, but they can avoid it by keeping track of financial and business events, news, and economic calendars. For example, stock markets are very sensitive to the central banks' rate policies and become highly volatile on those days. Nobody knows what kind of policy any central bank will adopt in its monetary meeting. But day traders can check the economic calendar and know which day these meetings will take place. They can avoid trading on those days and reduce the risk of loss in trading.

Therefore, knowledge of stock markets and being aware of what is happening in the financial world is essential for day traders. Many successful traders have a policy of staying away from trading on days when any major economic event will take place, or a major decision will be announced. For example, on the day when the result of an important election is declared, any big company's court case decision comes in, or a central banks' policy meeting takes place. On such days, speculative trading dominates stock markets and market risk is very high. Similarly, on a day when any company announces earnings results, its stock price fluctuates wildly, increasing the market risk in trading of that stock.

For inexperienced day traders, the best way to tackle market risk is to avoid trading on such days.

If you plan well, prepare your trading strategies before starting to trade; you increase the possibility of a stable trading practice, which can lead to profits. Therefore, it is essential to prepare your trading plans every day, create trading strategies, and follow your trading rules. These three things can make or break your day trading business. Professional day traders always plan their trades first and then trade their plans. This can be understood by an example of two imaginary traders. Suppose there are two traders, trading in the same stock market, trading the same stock. One of them has prepared his trading plan and knows when and how he will trade. The other trader has done no planning and is just sitting there, taking the on-the-spot decisions for buying or selling the stock. Who do you think will be more successful? The one who is well prepared, or the one who has no inkling of what he will do the next second?

The second risk management technique is using stop orders. Use these orders to decide to fix your stop -loss and profit booking points, which will take emotions out of your decision-making process and automatically cut the losses or book the profit for you.

Many a time, profitable trade turns into loss-making because markets change their trend, but traders do not exit their positions, hoping to increase profits. Therefore, it is necessary to keep a profit booking point and exit the profitable trades at that point. Keeping a fix profit booking point can also help you calculate your returns with every trade and help you avoid taking the unnecessary risk for further trades.

Taking emotions out of day trading is a very important requirement for profitable trading. Do not prejudge the trend in stock markets, which many day traders do and trade against markets, ending with losses.

Using Risk-Reward Ratio

Day trading is done for financial rewards, and the good thing is, you can always calculate how much risk you take on every trade and how much reward you can expect. The risk-reward ratio represents the expected reward and expected risk traders can earn on the investment of every dollar.

The risk-reward ratio can excellently indicate your potential profits and potential loss, which can help you in managing your investment capital. For example, a trade with the risk-reward ratio of 1:4 shows that at the risk of $1, the trade has the potential of returning $4. Professional traders advise not to take any trade, which has a risk-reward ratio lower than 1:3. This indicates, the trader can expect the investment to be $1, and the potential profit $3.

Expert traders use this method for planning, which trade will be more profitable and take only those trades. Technical charting is a good technique to decide the risk-reward ratio of any trade by plotting the price moment from support to resistance levels. For example, if a stock has a support level at $20, it will probably rise from that level because many traders are likely to buy it at support levels. After finding out a potential support level, traders try to spot the nearby resistance level where the rising price is expected to pause. Suppose a technical level is appearing at $60. So, the trader can buy at $20 and exit when the price reaches $60. If everything goes right, he can risk $20 to reap a reward of $60. In this trade, the risk-reward ratio will be 1:3.

By calculating the risk-reward ratio, traders can plan how much money they will need to invest, and how much reward they can expect to gain from any trade. This makes them cautious about money management and risk management.

Some traders have a flexible risk-reward ratio for trading, while others prefer to take trades only with a fixed risk-reward ratio. Keeping stop-loss in all trades also helps in managing the risk-reward ratio. Traders can calculate their trade entry point to stop-loss as the risk, and trade entry to profit as the reward. This way, they can find out if any trade has a bigger risk than the potential reward or a bigger reward than the potential risk. Choosing trades with bigger profits and smaller risks can increase the amount of profit over a period.

Using Your Trading Plan

Having a detailed trading plan is very important as it lays down some basic rules and guidelines, you're going to follow in your trading activities. This helps you manage your money and limit your exposure to risk. Your plan should include how much risk you're comfortable taking and how much capital you're going to invest. This way, you allocate a fixed amount to option trading and you never end up touching the money you can't afford to lose.

You can't eliminate emotions from trading, but what you can do is minimize the impact they have on your trades by putting rules in place. If you stick to your plan and use only the allocated amount of capital for trading, you avoid behaving irrationally and taking risks you can't afford to.

If you're generally conservative with your trades and it's been working fine for you, there's no reason for you to take higher risks suddenly. This is especially important when you make a few losing trades in a row. You might want to take a risky trade to recover past losses, but that's not a good idea. Remind yourself you have a trading plan in place for a reason.

Using Options Spreads

We've covered various types of spreads in the book. This is because they're one of the most powerful tools to dissipate your risk. Spreads let you combine different positions using the same underlying stocks, thereby helping you create a more secure overall position. The upfront costs to enter a position can be daunting, but you can use spreads to reduce them and thereby minimize the amount you stand to lose. Yes, it also reduces the potential profits you could make, but that's just part of controlling risk. We've covered several types of spreads in the book all ready to help you take advantage of pretty much any market condition.

For example, if you use a bull call spread, you reduce your initial investment and hence, limit the amount of money you stand to lose. This is done by buying ITM calls on a stock and then writing OOTM calls on the same stock since they're cheaper.

Similarly, when entering short positions, you can reduce your risk by using a bull put spread. This is done by writing ITM puts on a particular stock and then buying cheaper OOTM puts on the same stock by using some of that upfront payment you received from writing the put options.

As you can see, spreads are excellent strategies for risk management.

Portfolio Diversification

The most popular technique of risk management is Diversification. Investors using the buy and hold strategy are generally the users of this technique. The essence of diversification is spreading investments over various companies and sectors, thus creating an equitable portfolio of stocks instead of concentrating all the investment at a single point. This makes it less subjected to risk than a portfolio, which is largely composed of a particular type of investment.

Diversification isn't meant in the same way for options, but it has its uses. Diversification is used in options trading in different ways by using a combination of various strategies and trading options that have a multitude of underlying assets. The options being used can be of different types too. For using diversification, you just don't rely on a single outcome but create several ways of creating profits.

Using Options Orders

There's a range of orders you can use to manage your risk in a simple way. Besides the four main orders (buy-to-open, sell-to-close, sell-to-open, buy-to-close), there are a host of other orders we can use to manage our risk.

Let's see an example. It's typical for a market order to be filled automatically at the best price available, but this might not be a good price for you if the market is volatile. You can use limit orders here to set a minimum and maximum price. This way, you avoid selling or buying at a price you don't want to.

Similarly, you can use stop orders like market stop order or the limit stop order to control how you exit a position. This can help you avoid unmitigated losses or lock in profits you're comfortable cashing out at.

I advise you to read more about option orders once you have gained some experience in option trading.

Money Management and Position Sizing

Money management and risk management are closely entangled with each other.an investor has a certain amount available to invest, and hence it is crucial to control your capital budget. To not run into a position of inability to make more trades, one should take into consideration the size of a single position.

Position sizing means specifying the amount of capital you're willing to invest in a certain position. It's quite a simple tool to use. One must calculate what percent of their total invested capital is in each individual trade proposition. It is also kind of like diversification.

CHAPTER 7:

TRADING PSYCHOLOGY

An Options Trading Mindset

When it comes to making money trading options, it is important to remember that you must control your emotions at all times, which is easier said than done, especially if you are in the moment and have just taken an unexpected loss. Cultivating the proper mindset can be done with practice. However, and doing so will make it easier for you to face the early parts of your options trading career with the proper expectations in regards to what sort of results you can expect from options trading. Specifically, this means that you will need to understand that investing in options isn't a quick and easy path to success and, rather, is sure to take plenty of dedication and hard work if you hope to see reap the potential rewards.

The first step to finding success via options trading is to get your emotions in check. The best traders are robotic, they only rely on the facts and they follow their trading plan 100 percent of the time. If you find yourself getting extremely emotional as far as trading is concerned, then it is important that you start off by keeping a log of the emotions you have while trading and the results of those emotions on your trading outcome. While this might seem unnecessary at first, you will be surprised how helpful having a clear outline of your personal patterns is when it comes to improving your overall trade percentage in the long term.

The fact of the matter is that if you ever hope to successfully trade options, then you are going to need to know you can stick with your plan no matter what the emotional part of your mind is telling you to do. A good plan is one that remains successful, not 100 percent of the time, or even 95 percent of the time and instead manages to be successful roughly 60 percent of the time. While 60 percent is certainly enough to ensure you turn a profit, it is not enough that it allows for additional wiggle room in terms of letting your emotions talking you into going off the book at every turn. Remember, trading options is a numbers game and keeping your emotions in check is key to not working with skewed data.

Setting up a reasonable expectation

A trader who is staring up should always have the patience to wait to know a market and should not expect that he or she would a large and handsome profit from their trading options. A new trader should never high expectations when they are just into the market. Rather they should be mentally prepared for losing capital rather than gaining capital. A trader should always begin to expect at least a minimum market experience of a year or a half. This can be illustrated very simply in any field. A famous successful person always bears time and patience to be the greatest achiever in their field.

Proof concept

If a trader starts off with the small trade, he or she will not only gain experience but will also save time. Noises of the stock market do not affect the small traders, but if a trader starts with big trading options, he or she will react to these noises in the stock market. A new trader will be in a bad situation with such reactions and at the early time period. Starting with a small trade will teach a trader to manage capital, which is very much necessary. A trader remembers all trades are not the same in nature. A good trader will generate great ideas after the proper experience. A trader must always have records and check on them to see what idea works for them and what does not.

Proper sorting and record-keeping

A good successful trader should always keep a record of a few important things of the market like:

The trader should keep a record of orders placed and quantity involved in it and money-making out of it.

The trader should keep in mind implied volatility and its reference to the current condition.

The trader should keep in mind about his competitors in the market in that particular trade.

When the traders begin to keep a record and maintain records, they begin to move towards success and chances of being in an odd position is also reduced.

Good position of the trader

Once a trader has achieved his or her position in a trade or stock market, there are frequent ups and downs. A good position trader must know how to react to these situations. By small trade, he or she won't be much affected by the noise of the stock market.

The trader should keep in mind about buying stock exchange at the perfect time. When a trader does so, he or she can perfectly be in the market and understand well.

Proper evaluation of the position

A trader must decide very well that a few decisions like backing out on losses must be decided well according to the perfect time.

There are few other decisions like a plan suddenly executed and whether he or she should move on with the profit or go for more?

Even if the sudden plan does not work out then he or she must have a backup and move on forward ahead and not repent on his or her loss and look for a new fresh start.

Hard work is the only way to success

It's easy to advise and listen to it. But when it comes up to the execution of the advice it's not that easy as things do not turn up the way it's told.

The simple way is to start with small trade and have a lot of patience. A trader should do proper planning for execution. The trader should learn about the market and get into a good position and stick well to it and work very hard to achieve success and be a good disciplined successful trader.

At this point, it is time to move on to the next step. You already know some of the basics that come with working on options as well as some of their benefits.

If you want to become a successful trader who consistently earns a passive income time and again, you need to know how to navigate the psychology of trading. Anywhere you look, you will discover that the psychology of trading is as crucial to your success as virtually anything else and that a truly magnificent trader enforces this proper psychology.

Through fostering the right mindset and preparing your psychology for success, you can ensure that you are able to make the best trades possible, allowing you to maximize your profits.

The biggest reason why your mindset is so important when it comes to trading is that trading in and of itself can be incredibly stressful, and there is a lot at stake with each trade that you make. Although options trading is significantly less risky than other trading strategies, it is still risky and should be treated like any other form of trading to protect yourself against the risk.

When we become stressed during any life experience, our emotions have a tendency to hijack the experience and prevent us from being able to make logical rational decisions. Naturally, this would not be productive to you making the best decisions with your trades, which mean that this needs to be avoided at all costs.

Fostering the right mindset allows you to remain objective and logical in every trade decision that you make so that you are always making decisions that lead to your profits, rather than mistakes that lead to your losses.

It does take time to learn how to foster this particular mindset, especially with the amount of stress that you might face with trading. Ideally, however, if you practice at it every single day, you will find that it becomes a lot easier for you to see your trades objectively. As a result, you will find that your trades become more productive and your passive income stream grows exponentially.

While there are many things that you can do to help you manage your mindset and your emotions and keep yourself primed for the psychology of trading, there are five significant steps that you can take today to get started. Enforcing these mindset strategies right away can help you start your trades with the best mindset possible so that you can experience larger levels of success right from the very beginning.

Never take anything personally

In life, it can be challenging to separate yourself from your experiences, especially when high emotions such as stress and overwhelm come into play. Early on, you might feel like every trade you make reflects you personally and like any bad trade, you make means that you are a bad trader or that you are incapable of earning an income through trading. This type of response is fairly natural, but it is also unhelpful when it comes to learning how to trade to earn a profit.

Experiencing losses and trade deals gone wrong is a natural part of trading, and virtually everyone experiences it. While senior traders are not as likely to experience as ***many*** losses as new traders, they do still experience losses that cut into their bottom line. This is natural, especially when you are trading on something as volatile as the stock market. With day trading, in particular, you never know ***exactly*** how that day is going to go, nor do you know whether or not sudden shifts in news and rumors could completely change the direction of the stock. As such, you are certainly exposed to risks that can be completely beyond your control. While you can protect yourself against them as much as possible, there is no real way to completely avoid risks, and so they are always a possibility.

The alternative of feeling like a bad trader when you experience a loss is feeling like a great trader when you experience a win. It is common amongst new traders who are on a winning streak to develop a sense of indestructibility that suggests that maybe they are incapable of experiencing losses because they somehow have the system beat.

This arrogance can lead to new traders exposing themselves to massive risks and losses because they stop taking their trades as seriously and reduce the amount of researching and risk management they conduct before every trade. As a result, they may experience a massive setback due to this arrogance.

In either scenario, creating a personal attachment to what your trades "mean" about who you are as a person is not healthy. Both can lead to self-doubt or arrogance, which has the capacity to destroy your trade deals and reduce your effectiveness as a trader.

Instead, you need to go into every single trade deal, knowing that your level of results in the trades is not reflective of you as a person. You are neither good nor bad for participating in trades that earn profits or losses. You are just a trader, trading. Keeping your personal attachment out of the trades will help you stay objective and continually practice logic and rational reasoning in every single trade you make.

Always Stay Hungry for Knowledge

Trading is not a one and done skill that can be learned and then executed the same way over and over again without ever requiring further education on what you are doing. If you want to be a great trader and earn massive profits, you need to stay hungry for knowledge so that you can continually improve your trading skills over time. Despite the fact that the general rules of trading have always remained the same throughout history, there are several different factors that influence the market and how trades are being made. Over time you will learn more about technical indicators, how certain types of news tend to affect the market, and where the best sources of information are for you to learn more about your specific trades.

Chances are you will take what you learn here in this book and apply them, and over time you will find new information that helps you improve your trades even further.

It is important to understand that you should always be hungry and on the lookout for new information. Keeping your eyes and ears open ensures that you are always refining your practice and increasing your profitability in the market, which will, in turn, maximize your passive income. Every single person will have a different way of understanding the market, identifying important pieces of information, and preparing themselves for trades.

The best way to create your own method for doing all of this is to keep practicing and applying new strategies that you learn about as you go and seeing how they fit for you. When you find ones you like and that work for you, continue using them and refining them so that they work even better over time.

CONCLUSION

I hope this book was able to fulfill its purpose and help you understand what options trading is all about. Make sure you take the time to understand all the concepts covered in this book and then actually implement them in real life. If you don't put this knowledge you've gained to practice, you will forget it, and it would've all been just a waste of time. Remember to be patient, manage your risk, and keep learning more as you gain experience in the market. That's what makes a good trader.

The next step is to stop reading already and to get ready to get started taking advantage of the benefits that are unique to the options market. While it may not be exciting, what this means in practical terms is that it is time for you to get down to business and start doing your homework.

There is so much potential for making a profit when you work in options, but you have to come up with a plan and stick with it if you want a chance for success. This guidebook will help you to reach that success so that you can limit your risks and make as much money as possible with options.

Thanks for reading!

www.ingramcontent.com/pod-product-compliance
Lightning Source LLC
Chambersburg PA
CBHW070639220526
45466CB00001B/237